THE SEVEN TRUMPETS OF REVELATION

Recognizing and Surviving the Coming Crisis

Marvin Moore

TEACH Services, Inc.
P U B L I S H I N G
www.TEACHServices.com • (800) 367-1844

World rights reserved. This book or any portion thereof may not be copied or reproduced in any form or manner whatever, except as provided by law, without the written permission of the publisher, except by a reviewer who may quote brief passages in a review.

The author assumes full responsibility for the accuracy of all facts, cited quotations, and interpretations in this book. The opinions expressed in this book are the author's personal views and interpretations, and do not necessarily reflect those of the publisher.

This book is provided with the understanding that the publisher is not engaged in giving spiritual, legal, medical, or other professional advice. If authoritative advice is needed, the reader should seek the counsel of a competent professional.

Copyright © 2025 Marvin Moore
Copyright © 2025 TEACH Services, Inc.
Published in Calhoun, Georgia, USA
ISBN-13: 978-1-4796-1524-7 (Paperback)
ISBN-13: 978-1-4796-1525-4 (ePub)
Library of Congress Control Number: 2025911822

Unless otherwise indicated, all scriptures are quoted from THE HOLY BIBLE, NEW INTERNATIONAL VERSION®, NIV® Copyright © 1973, 1978, 1984, 2011 by Biblica, Inc.® Used by permission. All rights reserved worldwide.

Scripture quotations marked CSB are taken from The Christian Standard Bible. Copyright © 2017 by Holman Bible Publishers. Used by permission. Christian Standard Bible®, and CSB® are federally registered trademarks of Holman Bible Publishers, all rights reserved.

Scripture quotations marked KJV are taken from the King James Version. Public Domain.

Scripture quotations marked NCB are taken from the SAINT JOSEPH NEW CATHOLIC BIBLE® Copyright © 2019 by Catholic Book Publishing Corp. Used with permission. All rights reserved.

Scripture quotations marked NKJV are taken from the New King James Version®. Copyright © 1982 by Thomas Nelson. Used by permission. All rights reserved.

Scripture quotations marked NRSV are taken from the New Revised Standard Version Bible: Anglicized Edition, copyright © 1989, 1995 the Division of Christian Education of the National Council of the Churches of Christ in the United States of America. Used by permission. All rights reserved.

Published by

TEACH Services, Inc.
PUBLISHING
www.TEACHServices.com • (800) 367-1844

Table of Contents

Foreword	vii
Introduction	9
Chapter 1 Interpreting Symbolic Prophecy—Part 1	11
Literal or Symbolic?	11
Identifying the Meaning of Apocalyptic Symbols	13
Chapter 2 Interpreting Symbolic Prophecy—Part 2	17
Daniel's Prophecies	18
Revelation's Prophecies	21
Ellen White on the Churches, Seals, and Trumpets	25
Chapter 3 What Are the Trumpets, Anyway?	29
The Framework of the Trumpets	29
An Overview for General Impressions	31
What Do the Trumpets Mean?	33
Chapter 4 The Close of Probation—Part 1	37
The Setting for the Seventh Seal	38
The Censer Scene	40
Close of Probation in Revelation 15	43
Chapter 5 The Closer of Probation—Part 2	47
The Close of Probation in Revelation 9	47
The Interlude	48
Probation's Close as a Process	48
Chapter 6 The Coming Great Calamity	51
Before the Close of Probation	53

A Change in God's Dealings with the World	54
Balls of Fire	56
A Sudden, Unlooked-for Calamity	56

Chapter 7 God Uses the Forces of Nature — 59

Massive Destruction in Earth's History	60
God Uses the Heavenly Bodies	62
Signs in the Heavenly Bodies in the New Testament	63

Chapter 8 The First Four Trumpets — 67

The Cause of the First Four Trumpets	70
Comets, Asteroids, and Meteorites	72
The First Trumpet	73
The Second Trumpet	75
The Third Trumpet	77
The Fourth Trumpet	77
Conclusion	78

Chapter 9 Aftermath of the First Four Trumpets — 81

Chapter 10 The Fifth Trumpet — 87

The Star That Had Fallen from the Sky	88
The Abyss	89
The Locusts	91
How Will Satan Appear?	94
The Time Period	95

Chapter 11 The Sixth Trumpet — 97

The Four Angels	98
The Great War	99

Table of Contents   v

Chapter 12 The Mighty Angel of Revelation 10 — **101**

  The Mighty Angel Who Comes Down from Heaven — 102

  The Final Proclamation of the Gospel — 104

  Overview of Revelation 10 — 107

Chapter 13 My Understanding of the Two Witnesses — **109**

  The Two Witnesses and the First Six Trumpets — 111

  The Power of the Two Witnesses — 115

  The Testimony of the Two Witnesses Ends — 116

Chapter 14 The Two Time Periods of Revelation 11 — **119**

  The Time Periods in Revelation 11:2, 3 — 120

  The Time Period in Revelation 13:5 — 121

  Conclusion — 127

Chapter 15 What Ellen White Said About the First Six Trumpets — **129**

  The First of the Trumpets — 130

  The Fifth and Sixth Trumpets — 130

  My Response — 135

  The Interlude — 137

Chapter 16 What Ellen White Said About Prophetic Time — **141**

  Definite Time — 141

  The Two Time Periods of Revelation 11:2, 3 — 143

  My Conclusion — 148

Chapter 17 The Seventh Trumpet — **148**

  The First Segment of the Grand Ceremony:
  The Loud Voice in Heaven — 149

  The Second Segment of the Grand Ceremony:
  The Song of the Twenty-four Elders — 151

The Third Segment of the Grand Ceremony:
Throwing Open Heaven's Most Holy Place   152

Chapter 18 Putting the Pieces Together   155

    The Silence in Heaven   156

    The Trumpets   156

    Comparing Chronologies   157

Chapter 19 Getting Ready for the Events of the Trumpets   161

    Physical Preparation   163

    Mental Preparation   164

    Character Development   165

    Spiritual Preparation for the End Times   170

Appendix A End-Time Disasters Are Allowed
by God, but Caused by Satan   175

Appendix B Is the Land Beast the United States? (Rev. 13:11)   179

Appendix C The Seal of God   181

Foreword

This book has been a long time "incubating"—since long before Marvin began writing. It deals with a number of topics related to the seven trumpets, even if not directly so; topics like:

- The wrath of God
- Does God *cause* or *allow* disasters?
- God taking responsibility for disasters
- Close or closing of probation
- How to interpret prophetic symbols

Each chapter is important and builds on the previous one. The meat of the book comes in chapters 8-11, and the last chapter is also very important.

Marvin passed away in 2021. I know how important he felt this book was, and I share that conviction. Therefore, a good friend, C.M., and I have undertaken the proofreading and editing needed to complete it.

We have tried to preserve Marvin's thoughts and writing style, but if you detect a voice here and there that differs, it's because we sought to clarify a thought or found some inconsistency (which Marvin would have corrected had he lived long enough to edit it himself). Also, since his death obviously occurred before the horrific hurricanes and tornadoes of 2024, remember as you read this book that most of its contents were written several years ago.

This book will require careful study. Please pray for God's guidance. We encourage you to keep your Bible with you so that you can check it for *your* interpretation under the Holy Spirit's guidance.

–Lois Moore, June 1, 2025

Introduction

The ideas about the seven trumpets that I will share with you in this book first occurred to me back in the late 1980s. And I can still remember that it made immediate good sense to me, much more so than did the traditional Adventist interpretation, which seemed to me to be quite speculative—what I'd call "guesswork." I spent the next year or two studying the topic and developing the basic understanding I will share with you in this book. In the early 1990s, I wrote a 110-page, single-spaced manuscript, which I shared with people who requested it; and at first, I received quite a number of requests. Over the years, those requests dwindled to the point that today I receive only an occasional request.

> **Whether you agree or disagree with my conclusions, go back to your Bible and pray for the Holy Spirit's enlightenment.**

However, my interest in the topic has never faded. In early January 2020, having completed and submitted a book manuscript on the 144,000 to Pacific Press, I felt strongly impressed that it was time to update the original manuscript. The pages you are holding in your hands are the result of that update. It took me about six months to produce.

The trumpets are not included among our 28 Fundamental Beliefs, so I have no problem writing and sharing my thoughts on the topic. I believe our insights and interpretation of the Bible need to continually grow. Whether you agree or disagree with my conclusions, go back to your Bible and pray for the Holy Spirit's enlightenment (Phil. 3:15). That's how we all grow in our spiritual understanding.

–Marvin Moore
July 1, 2020

Chapter 1

Interpreting Symbolic Prophecy—Part 1

Apocalyptic prophecy is filled with terrifying beasts: a women riding on a leopard, locusts flying out of a great abyss, and vultures eating the flesh of merchants and generals. What do these things mean? How can anyone ever interpret them? How can we make sense out of the seven trumpets in Revelation 8–11? I have devoted the first two chapters of this book to explaining how to interpret apocalyptic prophecy.

I believe interpreting Revelation is not as difficult as we are inclined to fear when we first read these symbols. In this chapter, I would like to introduce you to the basic methods I use for interpreting Revelation's symbols. I find that as I apply these principles and follow these rules, Revelation opens up to me and begins to make sense. I'm sharing these methods with you at the beginning of this book because you will see me use them as we go through our study of the seven trumpets. I believe if you are aware of the principles I use for interpreting apocalyptic prophecy, you will find it easier to understand what I am saying.

I would like to discuss three things about interpreting the prophecies of Daniel and Revelation. First, how can we tell whether an idea in a particular prophecy should be interpreted literally or symbolically? Second, when an idea is clearly a symbol, how can we tell what it means? And third, how do we know the structure to bring to a prophecy, the framework into which it should be placed, and by which to interpret it?

Literal or symbolic?

Revelation 6:9–11 describes a group of "souls" under an altar crying for vengeance on their persecutors. The next five verses describe a great earthquake, stars falling to the earth, and terrified people all over the world hiding in rocks and mountains and begging the mountains to fall on them. Are we to understand these ideas literally? Adventists have generally understood the souls under the altar to be symbolic and the earthquake, falling stars, and terrified people to be literal, but how do we know?

I answer that question by starting with the literal. I ask myself, 'Has this happened or could it happen in real life?' If so, then I interpret the prophecy literally, at least initially, until I find some good reason for deciding it is symbolic after all. If it would obviously be impossible for a particular specification in the prophecy to be literal, then I conclude it is symbolic and try to interpret it that way.

> The language of the Bible should be explained according to its obvious meaning, unless a symbol or figure is employed.[1]

> Every declaration [of Scripture] is to be taken in its most obvious and literal sense, except where the context and the well-known laws of language show that the terms are figurative, and not literal; and whatever is figurative must be explained by other portions of the Bible which are literal.[2]

> The basic principle of biblical interpretation is to take words in their literal sense unless there is an unmistakable contextual indication to the contrary.[3]

The example of the souls under the altar from Revelation 6:9–11 that I shared with you earlier illustrates the point I'm making. It would obviously be outside the range of normal human experience to see dead souls caged up under an altar and crying for vengeance on their persecutors. I have no trouble concluding that this detail in the prophecy is symbolic. On the other hand, the earthquakes and star showers described in the sixth seal (see verses 12, 13) are natural events that have happened and will continue to happen in our human experience, and Seventh-day Adventists have appropriately interpreted them as literal. And while we don't normally see people so terrified that they beg for the rocks and mountains to fall on them (see verses 15–17), we know this can easily happen in an event as dramatic as Christ's second coming, which is the context in which these people are crying out.

---

1   Ellen G. White, *The Great Controversy* (Boise, Idaho: Pacific Press Publishing Association, 1911), p. 599.
2   Uriah Smith, *Daniel and the Revelation* (Nashville, TN: Southern Publishing Association, 1897), p. 4; cited by Don F. Neufeld in "Biblical Interpretation in the Advent Movement," *A Symposium on Biblical Hermeneutics* (Washington, DC: Biblical Research Institute, copyright by the General Conference of Seventh-day Adventists, 1974), p. 114.
3   Ibid., p. 176.

I will also point out that even when a particular specification in a prophecy is symbolic, in most cases, only the part that *does* the acting is symbolic. The activity itself and the result thereof are usually literal. For example, the little horn of Daniel 7 is obviously symbolic because nobody ever saw a horn with eyes and a mouth that talked. However, the little horn's activities were fulfilled literally by the papacy during the Middle Ages. The little horn blasphemed God, and the papacy did that—literally—with their claim that the pope is the vicar of Christ.[4] The little horn made war against God's people, and the papacy persecuted God's people—literally. The little horn tried to change times and laws, and the papacy did that—literally.

Identifying the Meaning of Apocalyptic Symbols

I pointed out in the previous section that when we say a particular specification in a prophecy is symbolic—a horn, beast, or star—we know it stands for something else. The specification itself is not real, but the thing for which it stands is. The question is, How can we identify the reality behind the symbol? I have found several ways to do that, which I will share with you here.

An overview for general impressions. I like to begin my study of a particular apocalyptic prophecy by looking at the prophecy as a whole to see if I can get some initial impressions. For instance, reading through the description of the little horn in Daniel 7, I notice it attacks God, His law, and His people. Even without understanding anything about the symbol, I come away with the distinct impression that the little horn is an evil power.

This general overview usually is not enough to begin identifying the exact reality behind the symbols, but it points us in a general direction. In the next chapter, we will look at the seven trumpets in this general sort of way.

From their definition in the prophecy itself. Sometimes, a prophecy will define its own symbols. Thus, we learn that the dragon in Revelation 12:7–9 represents Satan; the waters in Revelation 17:1 represent "peoples, multitudes, nations and languages" (see verse 15); and the beasts in Daniel 7:1–8 are nations (see Dan. 7:17). Because these symbols are defined in

---

4 A person blasphemes God when he or she claims to be God. The word "vicar" comes from the same Latin word from which we get our term "vice president." A vice president functions as president in the absence of the president. Therefore, for the papacy to say the pope is the vicar of Christ is to say the pope functions as Christ in His absence, and that's blasphemy because Jesus told us very plainly that the Holy Spirit would be His representative on earth in His absence (see John 14:16, 17).

the same vision in which they are used, we are left in no doubt about what they mean. In fact, we can sometimes apply the definition of a symbol in one apocalyptic prophecy to another one elsewhere. For example, knowing that water symbolizes peoples, multitudes, nations, and languages, we can apply that to the sea in both Revelation 13:1, from which the ten-horned beast arises, and Daniel 7:2, from which the four beasts arise. That's why Seventh-day Adventists have said these beasts arise out of populated areas, in contrast to the lamb-like beast in Revelation 13:11 that arises out of the North American continent, which, at the time Europeans first crossed the ocean to these shores, was largely unsettled.

Ideas from the world around us. Sometimes, it's possible to identify a symbol from its ordinary meaning in everyday life. For example, in Revelation 13:1, we see a beast rising out of the sea that has ten horns, and on its horns are ten crowns. Crowns are an obvious symbol of political power, and that is almost certainly what they mean in Bible prophecy,[5] unless there is a good reason to interpret them another way. A number of the symbols in apocalyptic prophecy were probably understandable to the people in Bible times because they saw these things used in their everyday lives. Our lifestyle is quite different from theirs, and symbols that would have been readily apparent to them may not be so apparent to us because we don't see them in our everyday lives the way they did.

Scripture parallels. One of the best ways to determine what an apocalyptic symbol means is to find parallels to it in other parts of the Bible. For example, in Revelation 1:12, 13, we see Jesus among seven golden lampstands, and in 4:5, we see God's throne before seven lampstands. We know Moses' tabernacle, which represented God's great sanctuary in heaven, had a lampstand (Heb. 9:2; Exod. 25:31-40). Thus, when we see the risen and ascended Jesus walking among seven golden lampstands (see Rev. 1:12) and God the Father on His throne, before which were seven lampstands (see Rev. 4:5), we know we are seeing them in the heavenly sanctuary.

From the symbol's activity. I mentioned earlier that in most cases, only the object that does something is symbolic. The activity itself is usually literal. Thus, one way to identify the meaning of a symbol is to ask, What entity in real life has done or might do the things the symbol does? For instance, if we were trying to figure out the identity of the little horn in Daniel 7, we could ask, What real power in the world has blasphemed God, persecuted His people, and tried to change His laws? If this matches one or

---

5   See Ranko Stefanovic, *The Revelation of Jesus Christ: Commentary on the Book of Revelation* (Berrien Springs, MI: Andrews University Press, 2009), p. 413.

more of the other ways in which we've been able to the identity the meaning of the symbol, that strengthens our conclusion.

There's one other issue we need to understand before I get into the actual discussion of the seven trumpets, and that is the overall method we will use to interpret apocalyptic prophecy. This will be the subject of the next chapter.

Chapter 2

Interpreting Symbolic Prophecy—Part 2

Students of the apocalyptic prophecies of Daniel and Revelation have typically used three primary interpretive methods: historicist, preterist, and futurist. I will briefly define all three for those who may not be familiar with them.

Historicism was the method adopted by nearly all the Protestant reformers of the sixteenth century. It was also the method of prophetic interpretation that was used by the Millerites and Seventh-day Adventist pioneers, and we have used it ever since. According to historicism as it's understood by Seventh-day Adventists, the symbolic prophecies of Daniel and the first half of Revelation are a brief outline of history from the time of the prophet to the time of the end. That's why this method of prophetic interpretation is called "historicism." In Daniel 2, the prophecy begins with Babylon and ends with Christ's second coming; in Daniel 7, it begins with Babylon and concludes with the judgment, which hands over dominion of the world to Christ; and in Daniel 8, it begins with Media-Persia and ends with the conclusion of the 2,300 days, which Seventh-day Adventists understand is when the judgment of Daniel 7:9, 10 begins. Daniel 9 begins with the restoration and rebuilding of Jerusalem and leads up to the arrival of the Messiah and His crucifixion.

Regarding Revelation, Seventh-day Adventists understand the seven churches, seven seals, and seven trumpets to begin with the establishment of the Christian church early in the first century A.D. and end at or near Christ's second coming.[6]

Preterism tends to be the favored interpretive method of liberal Christians. According to preterism, all the prophecies of Daniel and Revelation were fulfilled by the fourth or fifth centuries A.D. Daniel's prophecies of the four metals in the great image of chapter 2 and the four beasts of chapter 7 are interpreted historically as representing Babylon,

---

6   See Frank D. Nichol, ed. *The Seventh-day Adventist Bible Commentary*, vol. 7 (Washington, DC: Review and Herald Publishing House, 1957), Vol. 7, p. 788.

Media-Persia, Greece, and Rome. However, the little horn of Daniel 7 is said to represent one or more of the Roman emperors (Nero, Domitian, Diocletian, etc.), some of whom were persecutors of Christians during the first 300 years of the Christian era. Also, according to preterists, the beast powers of Revelation 13 represent these same persecuting Roman emperors, and they don't consider the seven churches, seals, and trumpets to have any—or perhaps very little—historical significance.

Futurism tends to be the preferred method of interpretation by conservative Christians, especially dispensationalists. According to this view, Daniel's prophecies about the metals in chapter 2 and the beasts in chapters 7 and 8 represent the great empires of ancient history, but futurists push everything after that into the distant future—to the time of the end, what they call "the tribulation." This creates a huge time gap between these ancient nations and the rest of Daniel's prophecies, which is the primary reason why Seventh-day Adventists reject futurism.

The origin of preterism and futurism. As I said a moment ago, the reformers of the sixteenth century were all, by and large, historicists. But the Roman Catholic system understandably resisted forcefully the prophetic interpretations that pointed to them as the diabolical little horn of Daniel 7 and the first beast power of Revelation 13. To counter this historicist interpretation, two Jesuit priests, Luis de Alcazar (1554–1613) and Francisco Ribera (1537–1591), came up with preterism and futurism, respectively, as alternate interpretations of Daniel and Revelation. Unfortunately, Protestants of almost all stripes have adopted one or the other of these two methods of interpretation. Today Seventh-day Adventists are about the only historicists left among Protestant prophetic interpreters.

Daniel's Prophecies

The historicist method of prophetic interpretation arises naturally in Daniel's great outline prophecies.

Daniel 2. I'm sure you're aware that in Daniel 2, the prophet interpreted a dream that King Nebuchadnezzar had of a great image that was made of four metals: gold, silver, bronze, and iron, as well as feet of iron and clay. And in verse 38, Daniel said to the king, "You are that head of gold." This clearly anchors the dream in history—the kingdom of Babylon—and if there should be any doubt about that, in the very next verse, Daniel said, "After you, another kingdom will arise, inferior to yours." That, of course, was the kingdom of Media-Persia. The next two metals represent Greece and Rome, respectively, and the feet and toes of iron and clay represent the nations of divided Europe from about the fifth century A.D. to the second coming of Christ. Christ's return is represented by the great stone that demolished the image.

Please note that the historicist method of interpretation is clearly evident in the very language Daniel used to explain the vision to the king.

Daniel 7. The same is true of Daniel's dream in chapter 7, in which he saw four great beasts arise from the sea: a lion, bear, leopard, and terrible beast that I like to identify as a dragon (see verses 1–7).[7] The dragon had ten horns on its head (see verse 7), but three of them were uprooted by an eleventh horn that grew up among them to make room for itself—something like the baby teeth in a small child that are pushed out by the adult teeth when the child is four, five, and six years old. Daniel said, "This horn had eyes like the eyes of a human being and a mouth that spoke boastfully" (verse 8).

All this was followed by a judgment scene in heaven over which God, "the Ancient of Days," presided, with the "jury" consisting of a huge host of angels (verses 9, 10). The result of this judgment was that "one like a son of man," undoubtedly Jesus, "approached the Ancient of Days and … was given authority, glory and sovereign power; all nations and peoples of every language worshiped him. His dominion is an everlasting dominion that will not pass away, and his kingdom is one that will never be destroyed" (verses 13, 14).

Daniel was quite mystified by this vision, so he "approached one of those standing there [no doubt an angel] and asked him the meaning of all this" (verse 16). The angel said, "The four great beasts are four kings that will arise from the earth" (verse 17).

Notice the pattern again: four beasts that represent four "kings" or kingdoms. Adventists, along with many other interpreters of Daniel's dream, have understood these four great beasts to represent the same kingdoms as did the four metals in the image of Daniel 2: Babylon, Media-Persia, Greece, and Rome; and that, to my mind, is a very reasonable, logical conclusion. Then the angel said something very interesting: "the holy people of the Most High [the Ancient of Days in verses 9 and 10] will receive the kingdom and will possess it forever—yes, forever and ever" (verse 18). In the vision part of this scenario, Daniel said "the son of man" would be given authority and everlasting dominion over the world (see verse 14), whereas

---

[7] The dragon beast of Daniel 7, which represents the Roman Empire, is not to be confused with the great dragon of Revelation 12, which represents Satan (see verse 9).

in the angel's explanation, the kingdom will be handed over to "the holy people of the Most High" (verse 18). I think most interpreters understand this to mean that in God's eternal kingdom, His people will rule alongside Jesus—something like the president of the United States governing the nation in cooperation with the Congress.

Finally, there's the boastful little horn that rose up among the other ten, uprooting three of them. Daniel 7:25 says this little horn will "speak against the Most High and oppress his holy people and try to change the set times and laws. The holy people will be delivered into his hands for a time, times and half a time." This is a prediction of the papal period of history that would last for 1,260 years, and that interpretation offended Catholics so much, it gave rise to preterism and futurism, which got the papacy off the hook.

Please note that all of this was history outlined in advance. The historicist method makes good sense in the interpretation of Daniel 7.

Daniel 8. This prophetic sequence begins with two domestic animals that are in conflict with each other: a ram and a goat; and Daniel's angel interpreter actually named the kingdoms they represented: Media-Persia and Greece (see verses 20, 21). Babylon is left out because at the time Daniel received this vision, it had almost reached its demise. Two primary interpretations have been suggested for the little horn that arose out of the goat's head. Most current interpreters have adopted the Antiochus Epiphanes view, which is history, but Seventh-day Adventists interpret this little horn as another description of papal power during the Middle Ages. The vision culminates with a prediction of 2,300 evenings and mornings (see verse 14), after which the sanctuary will be "cleansed" (KJV), "reconsecrated" (NIV), or "restored to its rightful state" (NRSV). Seventh-day Adventists are unique in understanding this "cleansing" or "reconsecration" of the sanctuary to refer to an investigative judgment in the heavenly sanctuary that began in 1844 and will culminate with the close of probation for every human being on planet Earth—an event which, at this point, is still future.

> **The historicist method is so obviously a continuous outline of history that I have a hard time understanding how anyone could miss it!**

Again, this is all history from the days of the prophet to the time of the end. It's the historicist method of interpreting Daniel's prophecies.

Daniel 9. Daniel's prophecies include predictions of three time periods: 1,260 days/years in chapter 7; 2,300 days/years in chapter 8; and 70 weeks or 490 years in chapter 9. However, Daniel 9 is unique in that it states the events that will mark both the beginning and the ending of the 69 weeks or 483 years: namely, the restoration and rebuilding of Jerusalem at the beginning and the arrival of the Messiah at the end (see verse 25).

Again, *Daniel 8 exemplifies the historicist method—history outlined in advance.* The historicist method in Daniel 2, 7, 8, and 9 is so obviously a continuous outline of history that I have a hard time understanding how anyone could miss it other than as a way to avoid implicating one's own church, which Protestants don't need to do!

Revelation's Prophecies

Now we come to Revelation and find a striking similarity to Daniel in the first half of the book. Just as Daniel 2 has a *sequence* of metals pointing to Babylon, Media-Persia, Greece, Rome, so in Revelation, we have a *sequence* of seven churches. Just as Daniel 7 has four great beasts pointing to those same ancient empires, so in Revelation, we have seven seals. And just as Daniel 8 has a ram and a goat representing Greece and Media-Persia, respectively, so in Revelation, we have seven trumpets. The conclusion by Adventist prophetic interpreters from the very beginning of our movement has been that these three prophecies in Revelation, like Daniel's prophecies, also represent periods of history.

However, there are also significant differences between Daniel's prophecies and those in Revelation. Revelation's prophecies, as we shall see, don't fit the historicist method quite as easily. I'll begin by sharing with you a significant observation with respect to the seven churches:

> The application of the various messages to the seven churches to seven consecutive periods of church history ... naturally suggests the utility of a series of transition dates to facilitate the coordination of the several messages with their respective historical periods. In attempting to assign such dates, however, it is well to remember that: (1) The prophecy of the seven churches is not a time prophecy in the usual sense of the term, for no specific chronological data accompany it. It is concerned primarily with successive experiences of the

church, and differs considerably from such prophecies as those concerning the 1260 of Daniel 7:25, the 2300 days ch. 8:14, and the 70 weeks of ch. 9:25. (2) Major eras of history can hardly be marked off by exact dates. So used, dates are at best convenient landmarks of a rather general sort, not exact boundary markers. Actual transition from one period to another is a gradual process.[8]

I will point out two things about this statement: First, note the second word in this paragraph, "application." In Daniel, the historicist method arises naturally out of the prophecies themselves, as we have seen. However, the historicist method does not arise naturally out of the messages to the seven churches. It has to be brought *to* the seven churches and *applied* to them. Second, the commentary clearly accepts the historicist method of interpreting the seven churches as the basic interpretive method, but it also acknowledges that that method is not as exact as it is in the interpretation of Daniel's prophecies in chapters 2, 7, 8, and 9.

Mervyn Maxwell adopted a similar, tentative application of the historicist method to the churches, seals, and trumpets in Revelation. "It is reasonable to *assume* that the prophecies in Revelation about the seven seals, the seven trumpets—and the seven churches—like the prophecies in Daniel, also parallel each other and that they run side by side from John's day to the end of the world."[9] Note Maxwell's somewhat cautious application of the historicist method to the interpretation of the churches, seals, and trumpets. He said it is "reasonable to *assume*" that method. And, of course, once that assumption is accepted, both of the previous sources proceed to interpret the churches, seals, and trumpets according to the assumed historicist method.

Yet the difficulty is evident even in their actual interpretation of these prophetic sequences. For example, regarding Revelation 6:1, one observation about the first seal is that "like the messages of the seven churches, the scenes revealed when the seals are opened *may be regarded* as having both a specific and a general application. … The scenes *may be viewed* as particularly significant phases in the history of the church on earth."[10]

Regarding the pale horse in the fourth seal, "*when applied* to a particular period of Christian history, the fourth horseman *seems to portray* a

---

[8] Nichol, *The Seventh-day Adventist Bible Commentary*, vol. 7, pp. 752, 753.
[9] Mervyn Maxwell, *God Cares: The Message of Revelation for You and Your Family*, vol. 2 (Boise, Idaho: Pacific Press Publishing Association, 1985), p. 92 (emphasis added).
[10] Nichol, p. 775 (emphasis added).

situation especially characteristic of the period from about 538 to 1517."[11] An observation about the trumpets suggests the sea in the second trumpet (see Rev. 8:8, 9) *"has been seen as* the depredations of the Vandals,"[12] and the great star that falls from the sky in the third trumpet (see verses 10, 11) *"has been interpreted as* portraying the ravages of the Huns under the leadership of their king *Atilla* in the 5th century."[13]

No such tentative interpretations are found regarding the symbols in Daniel's prophecies, and for good reason. In Daniel, the historicist interpretation arises *out of* the prophecies themselves, whereas in Revelation, it is *brought to* its prophecies and *applied to* them. This is especially true of the churches, where we find absolutely no suggestion of time periods. The seals have some elements of historical time. The first horse is reasonably interpreted as a description of the apostolic period, but the greatest evidence of a particular time is found in the sixth seal, which clearly describes the end time (the darkening of the sun and the falling of the stars) and the second coming of Christ, all of which will happen at a very definite point in time.

However, the best evidence of a sequence of events in Revelation is found in the trumpets, especially the last three. "Woe! Woe! Woe to the inhabitants of the earth, because of the trumpet blasts *about to be sounded by the other three angels!*" (Rev. 8:13, emphasis added). "The first woe is *past;* two other woes are *yet to come*" (Rev. 9:12, emphasis added). And if the last three trumpets have to do with time periods, it's reasonable to assume the same is true of the first four.

However, in spite of their obvious historical nature, the seven trumpets have proved to be very challenging for prophetic commentators. Jon Paulien, the dean of the School of Religion at Loma Linda University, wrote his doctoral dissertation for the Andrews University Theological Seminary on the first four trumpets and called this section "one of the most difficult passages in the Apocalypse."[14] And the tentative nature of many of his comments about these first four trumpets is indicative of that difficulty. For example, He said, "the thirds of the trumpets, therefore, *may represent* parts of Satan's kingdom which are brought under God's judgments"[15]; "the sea turning to blood [in the second trumpet] *probably*

---

11   *Ibid.*, p. 777 (emphasis added).
12   *Ibid.*, p. 789 (emphasis added).
13   *Ibid.* (emphasis added).
14   Jon Paulien, *Decoding Revelation's Trumpets: Literary Allusions and Interpretations of Revelation 8:7–12* (Berrien Springs, MI: Andrews University Press, 1987), p. 421.
15   *Ibid.*, p. 370.

represents a proleptic reversal of the persecution of God's people by the wicked mentioned in Revelation 16:4–6"[16]; and "the falling star which burns like a lamp [in the third trumpet] *probably symbolizes* the spiritual fall of the leading Christian teachers whose doctrines result in spiritual decline and death."[17]

I could keep going, but I believe I've made my point: There is a significant difference between interpreting the apocalyptic prophecies of Daniel 2, 7, 8, and 9 according to the historicist method and interpreting the apocalyptic prophecies in the first half of Revelation according to that same method. The historicist method arises naturally from Daniel's prophecies. It has to be *brought to* the prophecies in Revelation and *applied to* them. It does not arise naturally *from* them.

I don't mind *applying* the historicist method to the churches, seals, and trumpets, as almost all Seventh-day Adventist interpreters have done throughout our history, but is that the only valid way to interpret them? The answer is no. Adventist students of prophecy have typically used at least two other ways to interpret the churches, seals, and trumpets.

The spiritual interpretation. Seventh-day Adventists have always been aware that Christ's messages to the seven churches contain profound spiritual lessons that are applicable to all Christian churches throughout the ages of Christian history. However, the message to each church can also be applied to the spiritual experience of the Christian church at various times in history, which is the basis of the historicist method.

The message to the church in Ephesus, for example, is especially evident in the spiritual character of the church as a whole during the first century A.D., and the message to the church in Smyrna defines the spiritual experience of the Christian church circa A.D. 100–313, which was characterized by suffering under severe persecution. This is especially the case with the ten-year- period of 303–313, which aligns well with the angel's (or elder's) statement that the Christians living during that period would "suffer persecution for ten days" (Rev. 2:10). I'm fairly in agreement with our traditional *application* of the spiritual experience of the Christian church as a whole during the various periods of history. Certainly, the description of the church in Laodicea as lukewarm (Rev. 3:14–16) is characteristic of today's church, especially in the Western world.

The method of scriptural comparison. Many students of the churches, seals, and trumpets have also interpreted them through a comparison of

---

16 *Ibid.*, p. 383.
17 *Ibid.*, p. 403; see also pp. 371, 379, 382, 385, 394, 397, 405, etc.

their symbols with similar language in other parts of the Bible, especially the Old Testament. This method for determining the meaning of the various symbols in Revelation's outline prophecies is especially evident in Paulien's aforementioned dissertation.

Ellen White on the Churches, Seals, and Trumpets

Before concluding this examination of the historicist method of interpreting the seven churches, seals, and trumpets, we need to ask one other question: Did Ellen White say anything that would suggest the historicist method of interpreting the seven churches, seven seals, and seven trumpets? I looked up the terms "seven churches," "seven seals," and "seven trumpets" on the Ellen G. White website and will share with you below what I found.

The seven churches. I found eighty-four occurrences of the term "seven churches" in Ellen White's writings, and she did affirm the historicist interpretation of the seven churches in one clear statement:

> The names of the seven churches are symbolic of the church in different periods of the Christian era. The number 7 indicates completeness, and is symbolic of the fact that the messages extend to the end of time, while the symbols used reveal the condition of the church at different periods in the history of the world.[18]

It's clear, then, that Ellen White understood and accepted the historicist interpretation of the seven churches. However, what I also found is that throughout the rest of the eighty-four occurrences of the term "seven churches" in her writings, she commented on their spiritual importance. It's as though she understood and agreed with the historicist method, but for her, the spiritual value of God's messages to these churches was of paramount importance. What does the message to the church at Ephesus have to say to contemporary Seventh-day

> **" Smith focused on the historicist interpretation of the seven churches. White focused on the application of these messages to the spiritual life of God's people today. "**

18　White, *The Acts of the Apostles* (Mountain View, CA: Pacific Press Publishing Association, 1911), p. 585.

Adventists? What do the messages to the churches in Thyatira, Sardis, and Laodicea say to us today?

Uriah Smith focused almost exclusively on the historicist interpretation of the seven churches. He gave abundant evidence from history to show how the church and the world in each era fulfilled the details specified in the symbolic messages to those churches, and that's fine. Somebody needed to do that. However, as I said, in her comments about the seven churches, Ellen White focused her attention almost exclusively on the application of these messages to the *spiritual life* of God's people today. And she isn't the only one who did that. Ranko Stefanovic did so as well.[19]

For example, in his comments on the church in Ephesus he devoted seven pages to explaining the spiritual application of the message to the church in that city (Rev. 2:1–7), and a final paragraph on the eighth page titled "Historical Application" explained the traditional Adventist historicist interpretation. And he followed this pattern throughout his interpretation of each of the seven churches. I believe this was very appropriate.

The seven seals. My search for the term "seven seals" turned up six times in Ellen White's writings, two of which proved interesting. The first one I will share with you is as follows: "The vision as presented to John made its impression upon his mind. The destiny of every nation was contained in that book [sealed with seven seals]."[20]

At first glance, this appears to affirm the historicist interpretation of the seals, and perhaps that was her intent. However, notice she said, "the destiny of *every* nation was contained in that book," not the history of certain nations consecutively from the prophet's time to the end time. Ellen White's second comment on the seven seals that I will bring to your attention is similar to the first one:

> There in His open hand lay the book, the roll of the history of God's providences, the prophetic history of nations and the church. Herein was contained the divine utterances, His authority, His commandments, His laws, the whole symbolic counsel of the Eternal, and the history of all ruling powers in the nations. In symbolic language was contained in that roll the influence of every nation, tongue, and people from the beginning of earth's history to its close.[21,22]

---

19 See Stefanovic, pp. 114–121.
20 White, *Manuscript Releases*, vol. 12 (Silver Spring, MD: Ellen G. White Estate, 1990), p. 296.
21 White, *Manuscript Releases*, vol. 20 (Silver Spring, MD: Ellen G. White Estate, 1993), p. 197.
22 Compare White, *Christ's Object Lessons* (Washington, DC: Review and Herald Publishing Association, 1900), p. 244.

I will make a couple comments on this statement. Ellen White said the book sealed with seven seals contained "the prophetic history of nations and the church" and "the history of all ruling powers in the nations." Both of these sentence fragments can be understood to refer to the history of nations from John's time to the second coming of Christ. However, then comes this sentence: "In symbolic language was contained in that roll the influence of every nation, tongue, and people from the beginning of earth's history to its close." This isn't certain specific nations in consecutive order, nor is it from the prophet's time to the end of the world. It's *"every* nation, tongue, and people"; and it's *"from the beginning of earth's history* to its close." This is a significant modification of the historicist method.

The seven trumpets. The term "seven trumpets" occurs ten times in Ellen White's writings, most of which are about the seven trumpets of the priests who marched around Jericho following the entrance of the Israelites into Canaan. However, two of them are about the seven trumpets in Revelation:

> Thy right hand, O God, shall dash in pieces Thine enemies. Revelation 6 and 7 are full of meaning. Terrible are the judgments of God revealed. The seven angels stood before God to receive their commission. To them were given seven trumpets. The Lord was going forth to punish the inhabitants of the earth for their iniquity, and the earth was to disclose her blood and no more cover her slain....
>
> When the plagues of God shall come upon the earth, hail will fall upon the wicked about the weight of a talent.[23]

> "And when he had opened the seventh seal, there was silence in heaven about the space of half an hour. And I saw the seven angels which stood before God; and to them were given seven trumpets. And another angel came and stood at the altar having a golden censer; and there was given unto him much incense, that he should offer it with the prayers of all saints upon the golden altar which was before the throne of God. And the smoke of the incense, which came with the prayers of the saints, ascended up before God out of the angel's hand." [Revelation 8:1–4.] Consider this: No one humble, sincere prayer of faith [is] overlooked; every prayer is heard.[24]

---

23 White, *Manuscript Releases*, vol. 15 (Silver Spring, MD: Ellen G. White Estate, 1993), p. 219.
24 Ellen White, Lt 65, 1898. 23 (August 23, 1898) par. 24.

Both of these statements refer to the seven trumpets in Revelation, but the first one attributes these trumpets to Revelation 6 and 7, whereas the first mention of trumpets is actually in 8:2. The second statement is in the context of the sanctuary scene in 8:1–5, not the actual blowing of the trumpets in the rest of chapter 8 and all of chapter 9.

This review of Ellen White's comments on the seven churches, seven seals, and seven trumpets, while not as thorough as a doctoral dissertation would have to be, gives a general idea of her view of the historicist interpretation of these passages in Revelation. While she acknowledged that perspective, she made very little use of it. Her emphasis is almost entirely their spiritual relevance to Christians today.

This also concludes my understanding of the historicist method of interpreting the churches, seals, and trumpets in Revelation. While I recognize that Seventh-day Adventists have traditionally interpreted them that way, and I have no problem with affirming that interpretation, I have to recognize it is significantly less evident here than it is in Daniel, and therefore significantly less certain. And Ellen White's very limited acknowledgment of the historicist method in Revelation suggests to me that we, too, should be cautious about making too much of it.

Chapter 3

What Are the Trumpets, Anyway?

Imagine yourself a fairly well-informed Seventh-day Adventist who's familiar with our general understanding of end-time events: the latter rain, the final crisis, and the final warning, followed by the close of probation, the seven last plagues, and the second coming of Christ. You read Revelation several years ago and vaguely remember something about seven very strange trumpets, but you had no idea what they meant then and don't understand them any better now. Actually, you don't have to *imagine* that scenario. For most Adventists, that *is* the scenario. They really have no idea what the trumpets are all about.

I'm going to assume most of the readers of this book fall into that category and will walk you through the seven trumpets a step at a time, from start to finish. Unless you happen to have read through the seven trumpets recently, I suggest you do so now before you continue reading this book. You'll find them recorded in Revelation 8–11, with an interlude in chapter 10 and the first half of chapter 11.

The Framework of the Trumpets

Before getting into the trumpets, I'm going to review with you the basic framework of end-time events as it's understood by Seventh-day Adventists, because I'll be referring to it often in the remainder of this book.

When we humans organize things, we try to find a framework around which to organize them. For example, if you were to start a new library, one of the first things you'd have to decide would be whether to organize your books according to the Dewey Decimal System or the Library of Congress Classification. Each of these systems is a framework into which each book in your library can be placed.

In the affairs of everyday life, we're sometimes able to decide on the framework for a project before we begin organizing it. However, it's often necessary to study the material before deciding on the framework for organizing it. For example, a company hires a computer expert to prepare a program for its finances. The programmer has to spend many hours studying how the business operates before he or she can decide on the right framework around which to organize all the financial information. Only then can the expert write a program that will achieve what the company wants.

People who interpret prophecy usually have a framework around which they interpret it—a logical whole into which they fit the various pieces. Often, these frameworks are based on time. I believe it's a mistake to assume a particular framework will fit a particular prophecy and bring it *to* the prophecy before beginning to study it, just like it would be if a librarian decided ahead of time which cataloguing system to use. Rather, we should study the prophecy itself first and decide on the best framework according to what the prophecy itself suggests to us, the way a computer programmer studies a business before designing a program. We should let the framework arise *from* the prophecy itself. This is a very important principle.

In the next two chapters I'm going to develop a framework for interpreting the trumpets.

Even if you disagree with my conclusion, I believe you will see that I allow the framework to arise naturally out of what the prophecy itself says. I would like to share that framework with you now, ahead of time, because I think this will make it easier for you to understand what I'm doing as you read.

My framework is based on time. Specifically, my conclusion will be that the trumpets are end-time events. Once I have reached that conclusion, I will feel reasonably safe interpreting the trumpets in harmony with the general outline of last-day events that Seventh-day Adventists have understood for more than 150 years. Specifically, I refer to our understanding as expressed in the diagram below:

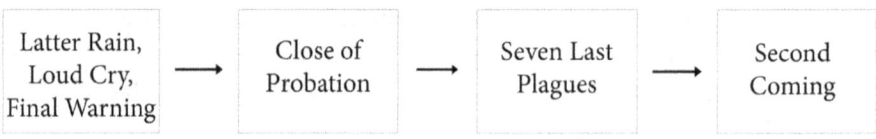

I'm going to assume most readers of this book are Seventh-day Adventists and reasonably familiar with this diagram. I find that the seven trumpets fit into this model the way a hand fits into a glove. And I believe by the time you have finished reading this book, even if you disagree with my conclusions, you will recognize their harmony with the traditional

Adventist view. The fact that the trumpets fit the traditional Adventist model of last-day events so well is, for me, one of the best pieces of evidence that the trumpets should be interpreted according to that model.

An Overview for General Impressions

In the previous chapter, I said I began my study of apocalyptic prophecy by reviewing the prophecy as a whole to see what kind of impression I got, so let's do that with Revelation's trumpets. The trumpets are strange, aren't they? Balls of fire falling on the earth; a horde of locusts with human faces and hair that looks like women's hair, flying out of a vast abyss in the ground; a huge army of 200 million mounted troops whose horses have tails like those of scorpions; and as though that weren't enough, millions of people die! If you wonder how anyone can make any sense out of that, you aren't alone.

Do Revelation 8–11 sound like words of comfort and hope? Are they about people worshiping God? Is this instruction a guide on how to raise children or a theological exposition on righteousness by faith? Obviously not! Even the most casual reading of the seven trumpets leaves one with the distinct impression that they deal with terrible catastrophes.

Furthermore, it's quite clear that these aren't just "natural" disasters. They are allowed by God and caused by Satan.[25] "I saw the seven angels who stand before God, and to them were given seven trumpets" (Rev. 8:2). God commands these angels to sound their trumpets, which means He proclaims the catastrophes these trumpets announce.

The Old Testament prophets also said God would send doom on the earth. Sometimes they said He would send the doom on His own people, who were rebelling: "[Jerusalem] must be punished; it is filled with oppression … Take warning, Jerusalem, or I [God] will turn away from you and make your land desolate so no one can live in it" (Jer. 6:6, 8).

At other times, the prophets predicted God would send disasters on those who oppressed His people. "'Babylon will be captured; Bel will be put to shame, Marduk filled with terror. Her images will be put to shame and her idols filled with terror.' A nation from the north will attack her and lay waste her land" (Jer. 50:2, 3).

---

[25] For further clarification, review Romans 1 and Ellen White, *The Great Controversy*, pp. 36, 589–590, 614.

As you read through the trumpets, do you get the impression God brings these terrible disasters on His own people or on the wicked? From the following verses, it seems fairly evident they fall on the wicked:

> [The locusts] were told not to harm the grass of the earth or any plant or tree, but only those people who did not have the seal of God on their foreheads .... The rest of mankind who were not killed by these plagues still did not repent of the work of their hands; they did not stop worshiping demons, and idols of gold, silver, bronze, stone and wood—idols that cannot see or hear or walk (Rev. 9:4, 20)

Therefore, just by looking at them carefully, before we identify even one symbol, we can tell the trumpets are disasters that God will allow the wicked to experience. And as you read through the seven trumpets, you will recognize something else quite interesting: the first six trumpets are in a group that's separate from the seventh. Between the sixth and seventh trumpets is an interlude—a long discourse—that includes chapter 10 (about a mighty angel) and the first half of chapter 11 (about two witnesses). We can diagram the seven trumpets like this:

Trumpet:	1 2 3 4 5 6	(Interlude)	7
Revelation reference:	8:6 to 9:21	10:1 to 11:14	11:15 to 19

Notice also that the seventh trumpet is distinctly different from the rest. As you read the seventh trumpet, you discover your eyes have shifted from terrible disasters on the earth to God's throne room in heaven. It begins with the announcement that Christ has taken over the kingdoms of this world, and He will reign forever and ever (see Rev. 11:15). We don't actually see the second coming of Christ, but it's announced. It's obviously about to happen.

When the twenty-four elders fall on their faces and worship God, they pronounce doom on the wicked, but we don't see that doom actually happening the way we did in the first six trumpets. It's announced. It's about to happen. And this announcement will be made in heaven.

This is probably about as far as we should try to go in understanding the seven trumpets just by reading through them. From here on, we'll have to interpret the symbols. Let's begin with the trumpets themselves.

What Do the Trumpets Mean?

As we look for the fulfillment of Revelation 8–11, we need not expect to see seven actual angels holding trumpets, nor will we hear their trumpet blasts. Rather, the trumpets are symbolic of something else. At this point, the question is not about what the seven trumpets in Revelation mean; it's about what any trumpet means as a symbol. The prophecy itself doesn't explain their meaning, but as you think about trumpets, what comes to your mind? I can tell you what comes to my mind: trumpets make a loud noise! They can be used to get people's attention. I have a very high level of concentration that's sometimes frustrating to my family. One of them will come into my office and say something, and I'll grunt and nod, but I'll be so engrossed in what I'm doing on my computer that what the person said doesn't register in my brain. On one occasion, my son was anxious to get my full attention, so he got out his trumpet, brought it into my office, held it fairly close to my ear, and blew. He got my attention!

> *Trumpets are loud! My son once wanted my full attention. He held a trumpet near my ear and blew. He got my attention!*

I believe in the same way, Revelation's seven trumpets mean God is trying to get the attention of the human race, but why? What does He want to tell us? To answer that question, we need to use the principle of scriptural parallels that I mentioned in a previous chapter. We need to look for uses of trumpets in the Bible to see if they give us any clues about what Revelation's seven trumpets might mean.

Had we lived in Bible times, we would undoubtedly have understood something about the symbolic meaning of trumpets in prophecy from the way they were used in everyday life back then. However, trumpets today are used in such different ways from their common use in Bible times that we probably won't get much help from our contemporary culture as we search for the meaning of Revelation's trumpets. Furthermore, John didn't define trumpets for us in his vision of the seven trumpets the way he defined the dragon as Satan in Revelation 12:9, 10. Nevertheless, we can learn a great deal by comparing Revelation's trumpets with references to trumpets in other parts of the Bible.

The New Testament mentions trumpets in only three contexts. One is the seven trumpets in Revelation, and since we're trying to learn about them in this book, we won't spend any more time there. The other uses of trumpets in the New Testament are with the resurrection of the righteous at Christ's second coming (see 1 Cor. 15:51, 52; 1 Thess. 4:16) and as signals in battle (1 Cor. 14:8). Trumpets in connection with the resurrection of the righteous don't seem to be much help in our search for the meaning of trumpets that are so obviously associated with disasters on the wicked, so we'll have to turn to the Old Testament for some clues as to the meaning of Revelation's seven trumpets. I will share with you four main uses of trumpets in the Old Testament; the first two seem to me to be particularly relevant to the trumpets in Revelation.

1. At the Feast of Trumpets. The Old Testament Jews celebrated about half-a-dozen religious holidays each year, one of which was the Feast of Trumpets (see Lev. 23:23–25; Num. 29:1). Throughout our entire history, Seventh-day Adventists have said the yearly feasts celebrated by the Jews in the spring of their year were a type of events in the plan of salvation that were associated with Christ's first coming, and the feasts in the fall corresponded to the events in the plan of salvation that immediately precede His second coming. The relevant feasts in the spring were Passover and Pentecost; those in the fall were the Feast of Trumpets, the Day of Atonement, and the Feast of Tabernacles. Our Seventh-day Adventist conclusion that Jesus entered the Most Holy Place of the heavenly sanctuary on October 22, 1844, to begin the heavenly day of atonement (the investigative judgment) is based on this analogy.

I believe Revelation's seven trumpets announce the approaching close of probation in the heavenly sanctuary the way the Jewish Feast of Trumpets announced the approach of the final cleansing from sin on the Day of Atonement in the earthly sanctuary.

2. To warn of impending disaster. Another very common use of the trumpet in Old Testament times was to warn people of impending disaster, especially of invading enemies. For example, Jeremiah said, "Sound the trumpet throughout the land ... Flee for safety without delay! For I am bringing disaster from the north, even terrible destruction" (Jer. 4:5, 6). Destruction from "the north" was the imminent invasion of the Babylonian armies, which would descend upon Israel from the north. Regarding this verse, "sound the trumpet" was to warn of impending doom (see also Jer. 6:1; 51:27; Ezek. 33:3, 6; Hosea 8:1; Joel 2:1; Amos

3:6; Zeph. 1:16).[26] Additionally, regarding Joel 2:1, trumpets are used to signal approaching danger.[27] In my opinion, the trumpet as a warning of impending danger and destruction is very useful to us in our study of the trumpets in Revelation. They are a warning to the human race that the armies of heaven are about to invade the world (see Rev. 19:11–16), and people need to repent of their sins.

3. *To call soldiers to battle* (see Num. 10:8, 9; 1 Sam. 13:3).

4. *To herald a new king* (see 1 Kings 1:34, 39; 2 Kings 9:13).

Now that we have looked at the four uses, let us return our attention to the uses which bear on our discussion here. I believe the trumpets are a warning of impending doom—the outpouring of God's unmingled wrath in the seven last plagues, and the second coming of Christ. They are God's way of getting the attention of the human race so He can warn us that we have very little time left in which to prepare for eternal life. People on earth won't literally *hear* these seven trumpet blasts. The disastrous events themselves will constitute "the trumpet blasts" that warn the world that God is about to intervene in human affairs by withdrawing His protection. These destructive events will be so terrible that even sinners will recognize that these catastrophes are supernatural.

I believe these disasters are near at hand and, to a great extent, they will be literally fulfilled. Frankly, there is no topic more relevant for Christians to study today than the seven trumpets of Revelation!

---

26 *The NIV Study Bible* (Grand Rapids, Michigan: Zondervan, 1985), p. 1126.
27 *Ibid.*, p. 1340.

Chapter 4

The Close of Probation—Part 1

The historicist method of prophetic interpretation is based on the concept that the majority of apocalyptic prophecies refer to real events that have happened or will happen in real historical time. Thus, one of the most critical questions anyone interpreting any of these prophecies must ask and answer is, When does this prophetic sequence begin, and when will it end? Identifying the correct time frame for the fulfillment of a prophecy is critical to understanding its true meaning. Those who identify the time incorrectly are likely to not only be unprepared for the events the prophecy predicts but also relate incorrectly to it in their own Christian experience and God's work on the earth in the present. Probably no better example of this can be found than the view during the Middle Ages that the Christian church was the eternal kingdom Daniel foretold would overthrow the kingdoms of the world (see Dan. 2:44; 7:14, 27). This led directly to the political supremacy of the papacy during the Middle Ages and the persecution of millions of innocent Christians by the Inquisition.

Therefore, in examining the trumpets in Revelation, it's imperative that we correctly identify the timeline when they will be fulfilled. We must especially search for evidence within the prophecy itself that can tell us when it was or will be fulfilled.

Seventh-day Adventists have traditionally interpreted the seven trumpets according to the historicist method. I pointed out in chapter 2 of this book that the historicist method understands the outline prophecies of Daniel 2, 7, and 8 to begin at the prophet's time and continue throughout history to the end time (see Dan. 7, 8) or the actual second coming of Christ (see Dan. 2). This interpretation arises naturally out of these prophecies. In Daniel chapter 2, for example, Daniel told King Nebuchadnezzar, "You are the head of gold" and "after you another kingdom will rise" (verses 38, 39).

However, I also pointed out in chapter 2 of this book that the historicist method does not arise naturally from the seven churches of Revelation, and the only truly historical aspect in the seals is the eschatological events of the end time in Revelation 6:12–14, including the falling of the stars, the darkening of the sun and moon, and a great earthquake. And all of these are followed by the second coming of Christ in verses 15–17. For the rest of the seals and the seven churches, the historicist method has to be *brought* and *applied to* them.

The seven trumpets clearly constitute a series of events, especially the three woes in Revelation 9. This is evident from three statements John himself made. "Woe! Woe! Woe to the inhabitants of the earth, because of the trumpet blasts *about to be sounded* by the other three angels!" (Rev. 8:13, emphasis added); and as the first two woes ended, the prophet said that one woe was past and the next two were coming (see Rev. 9:12; 11:14). This is clear evidence of historical progression, and I believe if the last three trumpets are sequential events, then it's reasonable to understand the first four trumpets to also be sequential events even though this conclusion isn't quite as evident in the text itself. My interpretation of the seven trumpets is based on the idea that they are descriptions of sequential events.

The question is, When do these sequences begin, and when will they end? I concluded a number of years ago that the trumpets are eschatological—that is, they predict the end-time events during the final crisis that will immediately precede Christ's second coming. The purpose of this chapter is to explain my reason for this conclusion. However, because Revelation 8 begins with the seventh seal, I need to start with a brief overview of the seven seals in Revelation 4–6 to give you the setting for this seventh seal, which in turn is the setting for the seven trumpets.

The Setting for the Seventh Seal

Revelation 4 opens with John seeing a door standing open in heaven and a voice that sounds like a trumpet calling to him, saying, "Come up here and I will show you what must take place after this" (verse 1). The rest of chapter 4 describes God's throne room in heaven. God is seated on His throne, surrounded by twenty-four other thrones on which are seated twenty-four elders (see verse 4).

Also surrounding the throne are four very strange creatures who praise God day and night (see verses 6–8). Now, any time you see God's throne room in the Bible, you can be sure that the topic is important. With that said, what's significant about this vision of God's throne room? Let's keep reading.

Revelation 5:1 continues this description of God's throne room. It tells of a mysterious scroll in God's right hand that John desperately wants to read. The problem is the scroll is sealed with seven seals. In ancient times, after a person had written a document on a scroll, he could roll it up, then seal it by dropping a bit of melted wax on the outer edge of the scroll and letting it harden. That way, if that person sent the scroll to someone, as long as the seal was intact when the recipient received it, he could be reasonably certain that the scroll hadn't been opened and read by some unauthorized person while it was on its way. Unfortunately, the scroll in God's right hand was sealed with *seven* seals, and nobody could be found in heaven or on earth who was qualified to break the seals and open the scroll (see verses 2, 3). John was deeply troubled by this. He "wept and wept because no one was found who was worthy to open the scroll or look inside" (verse 4).

Then, one of the twenty-four elders who was seated around God's throne said, "Do not weep! See, the Lion of the tribe of Judah, the root of David, has triumphed. He is able to open the scroll and its seven seals" (verse 5). The Lion of the tribe of Judah is, of course, Jesus, who conquered Satan and the prison house of death by His crucifixion, burial, and resurrection; therefore, He of all people should be qualified to open the scroll! The rest of chapter 5 continues with the twenty-four elders, the four living creatures, millions of angels, and all created beings praising Jesus for His victory on the cross.

This tells us the scroll has to do with the plan of salvation, which is the basic theme of the entire Bible. It's the theme of the universal conflict between good and evil that's been going on in our world for approximately 6,000 years—what we often refer to as "the great controversy."

Revelation 6 describes the opening of the first six seals. The first one depicts a victorious rider on a white horse who goes forth to conquer, but the next three show an increasing degeneracy into evil. The fifth seal describes God's persecuted saints calling out to Him for justice, and the sixth seal describes the terror of the wicked at Christ's second coming.

One of the lessons we can learn from what I've described so far is that God in heaven is in charge of the ultimate fate of the world. Evil may continue for a while, but Jesus Christ conquered the forces of evil by His death on the cross, and He and the Father will defeat them in the end. That, again, is the great controversy between good and evil.

Revelation 7 is an interlude between the sixth and seventh trumpets, and then comes the seventh seal in 8:1. It's a short verse that takes up only three lines in my NIV Bible: "When [Jesus] opened the seventh seal, there was silence in heaven for about half an hour."

This seventh seal has puzzled Adventist interpreters of Revelation throughout our history. What *is* this silence in heaven?

One source offers two possible interpretations. The first is the silence is caused by the absence of anyone in heaven during the period in which Christ is descending to this earth at His second coming. All the angels are with Him, as is God the Father (see Rev. 6:16, 17), so there's no one left in heaven to make a sound. This is probably the most common explanation of the silence in heaven. The second explanation regarding the silence in heaven is that it represents an expectancy of the awesome events that are about to occur—namely, the seven trumpets. I agree with the second interpretation. If the seven trumpets do indeed describe literal events in the future, then those events truly are awesome. They are a part of God's ultimate control of the world's history, guiding it toward its climax at Christ's second coming.

In fact, the very next thing to happen in Revelation 8:2 is that John sees "seven angels who stand before God, and to them were given seven trumpets," which suggests the seals and trumpets are closely related. Therefore, these trumpets are a critical part of God's grand plan to bring the conflict between good and evil to its conclusion. However, before the angels can blow their trumpets, something else of great importance has to happen in heaven.

The Censer Scene

One of the most significant clues that the trumpets are end-time events lies at the very beginning of that prophetic sequence:

> Another angel, who had a golden censer, came and stood at the altar. He was given much incense to offer, with the prayers of all God's people, on the golden altar in front of the throne. The smoke of the incense, together with the prayers of God's people, went up before God from the angel's hand. Then the angel took the censer, filled it with fire from the altar, and hurled it on the earth; and there came peals of thunder, rumblings, flashes of lightning, and an earthquake. (Rev. 8:3–5)

In order to understand this part of John's vision of the seven trumpets, we need to identify the altar from which the coals of fire are taken and know what a censer is and its purpose. I'll begin with the altar. There were two altars in the Old Testament sanctuary. One was the altar of sacrifice in the courtyard, and the other was the altar of incense in front of the veil that divided the Holy Place from the Most Holy Place. The altar in Revelation 8:3 is clearly the altar of incense in the heavenly sanctuary for two reasons. First, the angel takes coals of fire from the altar to put in his censer, in which he also places incense; and second, the altar is "before the throne." In the Old Testament sanctuary, the ark of the covenant was a type of God's throne in heaven, so the fact that this altar is "before the throne" is a clear indication that it's the altar of incense in the heavenly sanctuary.[28]

Next, we need to identify the censer in Revelation 8:3-5. Our modern censers consist of a small metal bowl that's suspended by three or four chains, and coals of fire and incense are placed in the bowl. The Greek Orthodox Church uses this kind of censer in its worship services. The priest walks through the church, chanting and swinging the censer, and the smoke from the incense leaves a sweet odor in the sanctuary. I believe censers in Bible times looked pretty much like these modern censers, and they were used in much the same way: coals of fire were placed in them. and incense was sprinkled on the coals, causing a sweet-smelling smoke to arise.

In the Old Testament, the censer is associated with the mediatorial ministry of the priests for the purpose of making atonement for the people. On the Day of Atonement, the high priest took a censer filled with burning coals of fire and two handfuls of incense directly into the Most Holy Place, and the smoke of the incense shielded the priest from the presence of the Lord that appeared between the two angels on the cover of the ark (see Lev. 16:13). And in the story of Korah, Dathan, and Abiram, when God began slaying the rebellious Israelites with a plague, Moses instructed Aaron to fill his censer with fire and incense and hurry out among the people, and "Aaron offered the incense and made atonement for them. He stood between the living and the dead, and the plague stopped" (Num. 16:48).

Thus, when Revelation says the angel used the censer in connection with ministering the prayers of the saints before God, it seems reasonable to understand this is a "snapshot" of Christ's mediatorial ministry in the heavenly sanctuary. Notice, however, that after the angel in Revelation 8:3-5 has

---

28   I'm not suggesting there is a literal altar of incense in the heavenly sanctuary. Revelation 8:2-5 is symbolic.

offered up the prayers of the saints, he again fills his censer with coals from the altar, but this time, he doesn't add incense. Instead, he hurls the censer onto the earth, and "there [come] peals of thunder, rumblings, flashes of lightning and an earthquake" (verse 5). And in the very next verse "the seven angels who had the seven trumpets prepared to sound them." Following this are the devastating disasters announced by the sounding of the trumpets.

The point is that the casting down of the censer preceded the sounding of the trumpets; indeed, it had to be cast down before the trumpets could sound. With that said, what does the casting down of the censer mean? If the censer was used in Old Testament times in connection with the temple ritual, and particularly for making atonement, then when the censer in the heavenly sanctuary is cast down, in some way, the atonement ministry in the heavenly sanctuary must have ended. There is support for this conclusion:

> The meaning of this act [casting down the censer] is significant for the understanding of what follows as the trumpets are blown ... According to the view that Seventh-day Adventists have favored, the cessation of the angel's ministry at the altar of incense is symbolic of the end of the ministration of Christ for mankind—the close of probation.[29]

This explains why some Seventh-day Adventists who interpret the judgments of the seven trumpets as end-time events understand they will be fulfilled *after* the close of probation. We can diagram it like this:

Close of Probation		Second Coming
	Seven trumpets sound	
Censer Cast down		

If the casting down of the censer is indeed a symbol of the cessation of Christ's ministry in the heavenly sanctuary, then the evidence seems compelling that the trumpets will sound after the close of probation. However,

---

29 Nichol, *The Seventh-day Adventist Bible Commentary*, vol. 7, p. 787.

after studying all the evidence carefully, I'm convinced that the seven trumpets will occur *before* the close of probation, like this:

Censer Cast down	Close of Probation	Second coming
Seven trumpets		Seven plagues

In the rest of this chapter, I will explain why I believe the first six trumpets precede the close of probation.

Close of Probation in Revelation 15

One of the most detailed discussions of the close of probation in the entire book of Revelation is found in chapter 15. John began by showing us the seven angels with the seven last plagues (see verse 1), but a quick check will show you that these angels do not begin to pour out the plagues until Revelation 16:1. They aren't *allowed* to pour out the plagues until all the events of chapter 15 have happened—events that are associated with the close of probation. The close of probation is particularly evident in verses 5 and 8, which we will now examine.

In Revelation 15:5, John gave us a glimpse into the Most Holy Place of the heavenly sanctuary: "After this, in my vision, the temple, that is, *the tabernacle of the Testimony, was opened*" (NCB, emphasis added). The key statement here is "the tabernacle of the Testimony

> **Christ's mediatorial ministry for sinners in the heavenly sanctuary has come to an end. And that is the close of probation.**

was opened." The closest analogy to this anywhere else in the Bible is the rending of the veil in the earthly sanctuary at the time Christ died, exposing the Most Holy Place (Luke 23:45, 46). By this, God indicated that the services in the earthly sanctuary had come to an end. The Jews continued to offer their sacrifices for almost forty years until the destruction of Jerusalem in A.D. 70, but as far as God was concerned, these sacrifices held no meaning after Christ's death. They were an empty ritual.

If the opening of the temple of God in heaven corresponds to the rending of the veil in the earthly sanctuary, which I believe it does, then Revelation 15:5 is telling us Christ's mediatorial ministry for sinners in the heavenly sanctuary has come to an end. And that is the close of probation.

Another obvious description of the close of probation in Revelation 15 is found in verse 8: "And the temple was filled with smoke from the glory of God and from his power, and no one could enter the temple until the seven plagues of the seven angels were completed." This verse says the temple had no people in it. That means Jesus could not be officiating as Mediator for sinners. This point becomes utterly clear when we compare Revelation 15:8 with a scene in the Old Testament on which John based his description of the empty temple. This scene occurred at the time Solomon dedicated his temple:

> When Solomon finished praying, fire came down from heaven and consumed the burnt offering and the sacrifices, and the glory of the LORD filled the temple. The priests could not enter the temple of the LORD because the glory of the LORD filled it (2 Chron. 7:1, 2).

Please notice four things about the dedication of Solomon's temple and compare them with the scene John described in Revelation 15:8:

Dedication of Solomon's Temple	The Temple in Revelation
1. A cloud filled the temple	1. Smoke filled the temple
2. The glory of the Lord filled the temple	2. The glory of the Lord filled the temple
3. The priests could not enter the temple	3. No one could enter the temple
4. The priests could not officiate in the temple	

The fourth point in the dedication of Solomon's temple isn't mentioned in Revelation, but the similarity to the other three is so close that it seems certain that the dedication of Solomon's temple is the model on which John based his description of the heavenly temple in Revelation 15:8. That being the case, we can apply to this verse the fact that the priests could not officiate while the temple was filled with a cloud and the glory of God; and we can say Christ will not be officiating as our Mediator for sinners in the heavenly sanctuary while the smoke and the glory of God fill the heavenly sanctuary.

This view fits perfectly with traditional Adventist eschatology. Adventists have always taught that the close of probation will occur a short time before the seven last plagues, and that is exactly when the sanctuary scene in Revelation 15:8 occurs. Indeed, the fact that the sanctuary scene immediately precedes the pouring out of the seven last plagues is another good reason to interpret 15:8 as the close of probation. Therefore, we can now diagram the seven trumpets and the seven last plagues like this:

There are yet other issues related to the close of probation that we need to discuss in order to fully understand the casting down of the censer in Revelation 8:5. These issues will be the topic of the next chapter.

Chapter 5

The Close of Probation—Part 2

In the previous chapter, I explained why the casting down of the censer is a close-of-probation scene, which is why some interpreters of the trumpets who view them as end-time events also believe they will take place after the close of probation.

The Close of Probation in Revelation 9

The censer scene isn't the only place within the unfolding of the seven trumpets where we find close-of-probation language. The sixth trumpet takes up the second half of Revelation 9 and describes a fierce battle that will involve 200 million troops (see verse 16), which is symbolic language.

> The rest of mankind that were not killed by these plagues still did not repent of the work of their hands; they did not stop worshiping demons and idols of gold, silver, bronze, stone and wood—idols that cannot see or hear or walk. *Nor did they repent* of their murders, their magic arts, their sexual immorality or their thefts. (Rev. 9:20, 21, emphasis added)

Now, compare this with a couple of statements by the angels who pour out the fourth and fifth plagues:

> The fourth angel poured out his bowl on the sun, and the sun was allowed to scorch people with fire. They were seared by the intense heat and they cursed the name of God, who had control over these plagues, *but they refused to repent* and glorify him.

> The fifth angel poured out his bowl on the throne of the beast, and its kingdom was plunged into darkness. People gnawed their tongues in agony and cursed the God of heaven because of their pains and their sores, *but they refused to repent* of what they had done. (Rev. 16:8–11, emphasis added)

Notice that at the end of the sixth trumpet, the wicked refuse to repent, and in the fourth and fifth plagues, the people also refuse to repent. This is a clear suggestion that the close of probation has happened.

The Interlude

The seals and trumpets share a unique characteristic: They each have an interlude between their sixth and seventh segments. With the seals, the interlude comes in Revelation 7 and consists of two parts: the 144,000 and the great multitude. With the trumpets, the interlude, like that between the seals, has two parts: In the first part, a mighty Angel descends from heaven in chapter 10; and in the second part (see Rev. 11:1–13), we learn about two witnesses who are severely persecuted. The seventh angel sounds his trumpet in Revelation 11:15–19. I will discuss this interlude in some detail in two later chapters. For now, it's enough to call your attention to verse 15: "The seventh angel sounded his trumpet, and there were loud voices in heaven, which said: 'The kingdom of the world has become the kingdom of our Lord and of his Messiah, and he will reign for ever and ever.'"

These words are strongly reminiscent of a proclamation in Daniel 7:14 at the conclusion of the judgment. The judgment declares that "a son of man," who is Christ, was given authority, glory, and sovereign power; all peoples, nations, and those of every language worshiped Him. His dominion is an everlasting dominion that will not pass away, and His kingdom is one that will never be destroyed.

Notice two similarities between these verses: first, both are about Christ receiving the kingdom and dominion; and second, in both cases, the kingdom lasts forever. Daniel makes it clear that this will happen as a result of the great judgment in heaven (see Dan. 7:9–14), which Seventh-day Adventists from almost the beginning of our history have called "the investigative judgment." When that judgment reaches its final verdict, probation will close.

Probation's Close as a Process

It helps to distinguish between the *closing* of probation as a process in time versus the *ending* of the process. The concept of the final *close* of probation could indicate that every soul on earth has made their final choice; that is, they are so convinced that they will never change their minds.

The idea of the closing of probation as a process is described in Revelation 7:3. Most Adventists probably agree that some people will make their final decision for or against God earlier than others will. If this is true, then in that sense, the *closing* of probation will occur over a period of time. Ellen White made this point clear:

> The time of God's destructive judgments is the time of mercy for those who have had no opportunity to learn what is truth. Tenderly will the Lord look upon them. His heart of mercy is touched; *His hand is still stretched out to save, while the door is closed to those who would not enter.*[30]

---

[30] White, *Christian Service* (Washington, DC: Review and Herald Publishing Association, 1925), p. 56 (emphasis added).

Chapter 6

The Coming Great Calamity

A careful examination of the evidence in the Bible has led me to an extremely significant conclusion: Terrible judgments in the form of natural disasters will come upon the world at the very end of time. We must always remember that they are allowed by God but caused by Satan (see Appendix A). Paul suggested this: "For you know very well that the day of the Lord will come like a thief in the night. While people are saying, 'Peace and safety,' destruction will come on them suddenly, as labor pains on a pregnant woman, and they will not escape" (1 Thess. 5:2, 3).

Paul was speaking about the second coming of Christ when he referred to "the day of the Lord." Revelation tells us that a terrible earthquake will devastate the world at Christ's second coming (see Rev. 6:12–14; 16:18, 20). However, Jesus made it clear that devastating natural disasters will occur *before* His coming as *signs* of His return. Luke was especially clear in the way he quoted Jesus on this point: "There will be signs in the sun, moon, and stars. On the earth, nations will be in anguish and perplexity at the roaring and tossing of the sea. Men will faint from terror, apprehensive of what is coming on the earth, for the heavenly bodies will be shaken" (Luke 21:25, 26).

Notice that Jesus said nations will be in "anguish" and "perplexity." Anguish means "this hurts a lot," and perplexity means "what do we do now?" Anguish and perplexity are what I (or anyone) would experience if I were to come home one day and find my house on fire. When Jesus said nations will be in anguish and perplexity, He was talking about the international community—in other words, the entire world.

Matthew's words are even more ominous than Luke's are: "For then there will be great distress, unequaled from the beginning of the world until now—and never to be equaled again. If those days had not been cut short, no one would survive, but for the sake of the elect those days will be shortened" (Matt. 24:21, 22; see also Dan. 12:1).

Jesus' statement that if earth's final time of trouble weren't cut short, "no one would survive," suggests the judgments that will come upon the world at that time will be so severe that the human race will be threatened with extinction. No wonder the nations will be in "anguish and perplexity"!

Ellen White also predicted that terrible natural disasters would come upon the world just before the second coming of Christ. The rest of this chapter is a compilation of her statements about these disasters. Following are several quotes that suggest there will be end-time disasters without giving us any clue as to when in the flow of final events they will happen:

> Earthquakes in various places have been felt, but these disturbances have been very limited.... Terrible shocks will come upon the earth, and the lordly palaces erected at great expense will certainly become heaps of ruins. The earth's crust will be rent by the outbursts of the elements concealed in the bowels of the earth.[31]

This statement suggests two kinds of well-known disasters: earthquakes ("terrible shocks will come upon the earth") and volcanoes ("earth's crust will be rent by the outbursts of the elements concealed in the bowels of the earth").

> [Quotes from Luke 21:25]. Yes, they [the sea and the waves] shall pass their borders, and destruction will be in their track. They will engulf the ships that sail upon their broad waters, and with the burden of their living freight, they will be hurried into eternity without time to repent.[32]

The idea of the sea and waves passing their borders suggests tidal waves, and a ship that was near the shore when the disaster happens would be swept into the catastrophe. "O that God's people had a sense of the impending destruction of thousands of cities, now almost given to idolatry."[33]

In the wake of Hurricane Andrew, which devastated Florida in 1992, only one city, Homestead, Florida, could be considered to have been totally destroyed,[34] but Ellen White said thousands of cities will be destroyed. "The time is near when large cities will be swept away, and all should be warned of these coming judgments. But who is giving to the accomplishment of this work the wholehearted service that God requires?"[35]

---

31 White, *Selected Messages*, book 3 (Washington, DC: Review and Herald Publishing Association, 1980), p. 391.
32 Ibid., p. 417.
33 White, *Last Day Events*, (Boise, Idaho: Pacific Press Publishing Association, 1992), p. 111.
34 See "Hurricane Andrew," Wikipedia Foundation, last modified June 16, 2022, 23:19. https://1ref.us/7t01.
35 White, *Evangelism* (Washington, DC: Review and Herald Publishing Association, 1946), p. 29.

The second sentence in this quote challenges us to be far more proactive in helping people to know Jesus so they are spiritually prepared for the disasters that are coming upon the world in the near future.

Before the Close of Probation

Many Adventists reading these statements would probably conclude that they refer to the seven last plagues after the close of probation. However, other statements by Ellen White make it clear that some of these allowed judgments will occur before probation closes as a warning to the human race that the end is near. I have emphasized the sentences in the following quotations that especially suggest the judgments allowed by God will also occur *before* the close of probation:

> During a vision of the night, I stood on an eminence, from which I could see houses shaken like a reed in the wind. Buildings, great and small, were falling to the ground. Pleasure resorts, theaters, hotels, and the homes of the wealthy were shaken and shattered. Many lives were blotted out of existence, and the air was filled with the shrieks of the injured and the terrified …
>
> … the awfulness of the scenes that passed before me I cannot find words to describe. It seemed that the forbearance of God was exhausted, and that the judgment day had come ….
>
> The angel that stood by my side declared that God's supreme rulership, and the sacredness of His law, must be revealed to those who persistently refuse to render obedience to the King of kings. *Those who choose to remain disloyal must be visited in mercy with judgments, in order that, if possible, they may be aroused to a realization of the sinfulness of their course.*[36]
>
> I am bidden to declare the message that cities full of transgression, and sinful in the extreme, will be destroyed by earthquakes, by fire, by flood ….
>
> Calamities will come—calamities most awful, most unexpected; and these destructions will follow one another ….

---

36 *Ibid.*, p. 28 (emphasis added).

> Strictly will the cities of the nations be dealt with, and yet they will not be visited in the extreme of God's indignation, because *some souls will yet break away from the delusions of the enemy, and will repent and be converted,* while the mass will be treasuring up wrath against the day of wrath.[37]

These disasters *have* to precede the close of probation because as a result of them, some people will repent and turn to God. That cannot happen after the close of probation. The same thought is expressed in the following statements:

> There are many souls to come out of the ranks of the world, out of the churches—even the Catholic Church—whose zeal will far exceed that of those who have stood in rank and file to proclaim the truth heretofore .... When the crisis is upon us, when the season of calamity shall come, *[the souls from other churches] will come to the front, gird themselves with the whole armor of God, and exalt His law.*[38]

> *The time of God's destructive judgments is the time of mercy for those who have [had] no opportunity to learn what is truth.* Tenderly will the Lord look upon them. His heart of mercy is touched; *His hand is still stretched out to save,* while the door is closed to those who would not enter.[39]

A Change in God's Dealings with the World

It's extremely important for a proper interpretation of the seven trumpets to understand that the coming judgments will be the result of God's response to those who refuse His protection.

> The angel that stood by my side ... declared that the Lord has appointed a time when He will visit transgressors in wrath for persistent disregard of His law.[40]

---

37 *Ibid.*, pp. 27, 28 (emphasis added).
38 White, *Selected Messages*, book 3, p. 386, 387 (emphasis added).
39 White, *Christian Service*, p. 56 (emphasis added).
40 White, *Testimonies for the Church*, vol. 9 (Mountain View, CA: Pacific Press Publishing Association, 1909), p. 93.

> When God's restraining hand is removed, the destroyer begins his work. Then in our cities the greatest calamities will come.[41]

> Do you believe that the Lord is coming, and that the last great crisis is about to break upon the world? There will soon come a sudden change in God's dealings. The world in its perversity is being visited by casualties,—by floods, storms, fires, earthquakes, famines, wars, and bloodshed. The Lord is slow to anger, and great in power ... but His forbearance will not always continue. Who is prepared for the sudden change that will come in God's dealing with sinful men?[42]

Notice that the context of this third statement is "the last great crisis" that is "about to break upon the world." This crisis will come as a result of "a sudden change" in the way God deals with the world. Ellen White said that even in her day, God's judgments were being felt in the world—floods, storms, earthquakes, etc.—"But who is prepared," she asked, "for the sudden change that will take place in God's dealings with sinful men?" Clearly, the terrible natural disasters that God allows Satan to bring upon the world when the final crisis begins had not started in her day, nor have they begun in ours. They will not begin until a "sudden change takes place in God's dealings with the world." My personal opinion is that this sudden change in God's dealings is foretold in Revelation by the casting down of the censer (Rev. 8:4, 5).

Balls of Fire

Ellen White made several startling references to great balls of fire falling on the earth:

> Last Friday morning, just before I awoke, a very impressive scene was presented before me. I seemed to awake from sleep but was not in my home. From the windows I could behold a terrible conflagration. Great balls of fire were falling upon houses, and from these balls fiery arrows were flying in every direction. It was impossible to check the fires that were kindled, and many places were destroyed. The terror of the people was indescribable.[43]

---

41 White, *Manuscript Releases* vol. 3, (Silver Spring, MD: Ellen G. White Estate, 1990), p. 314; see also *Last Day Events*, p. 111.
42 White, *Fundamentals of Christian Education* (Nashville, TN: Southern Publishing Association, 1923), pp. 356, 357.
43 White, *Evangelism*, p. 29.

In one instance, she spoke of "an immense ball of fire" falling on the world:

Last night a scene was presented before me. I may never feel free to reveal all of it, but I will reveal a little.

It seemed that an immense ball of fire came down upon the world, and crushed large houses. From place to place rose the cry, "The Lord has come! The Lord has come!" Many were unprepared to meet Him, but a few were saying, "Praise the Lord!"

"Why are you praising the Lord?" inquired those upon whom was coming sudden destruction.

"Because we now see what we have been looking for."

"If you believed that these things were coming, why did you not tell us?" was the terrible response. "We did not know about these things. Why did you leave us in ignorance? Again and again you have seen us; why did you not become acquainted with us, and tell us of the judgment to come, and that we must serve God, lest we perish. Now we are lost!"[44]

> *They will be much more likely to believe us after it's happened than they would have beforehand.*

This comment is certainly a challenge for us to share these things with our relatives, friends, and neighbors. I will point out, however, that the people who said, "Now we are lost" probably were not. In all probability, the scenario Ellen White described will occur before the close of probation as a warning judgment, which means even if we haven't told our friends and neighbors about it before, there's still time, and they will be much more likely to believe us after it's happened than they would have beforehand.

A Sudden, Unlooked-for Calamity

Ellen White made several startling statements about the coming crisis:

Transgression has almost reached its limit. Confusion fills the world, and a great terror is soon to come upon human beings. The end is very near. We who know the truth should be preparing for

---

44   White, *Reflecting Christ* (Hagerstown, MD: Review and Herald Publishing Association, 1985), p. 243.

what is soon to break upon the world as an *overwhelming surprise* (emphasis added).[45]

It is in a crisis that character is revealed. When the earnest voice proclaimed at midnight, "Behold the bridegroom cometh; go ye out to meet him," and the sleeping virgins were roused from their slumbers, it was seen who had made preparation for the event. Both parties were taken unawares; but one was prepared for the emergency, and the other was found without preparation. So now, a sudden and unlooked-for calamity, something that brings the soul face to face with death, will show whether there is any real faith in the promises of God. It will show whether the soul is sustained by grace. The great final test comes at the close of human probation, when it will be too late for the soul's need to be supplied.[46]

In both of these statements, the calamity is overwhelming and totally unexpected. Ellen White also spoke of the second one in the singular, which will mark the close of probation ("when it will be too late for the soul's need to be supplied"). This doesn't mean it will be the only natural disaster to come upon the world at that time. We already saw there will be many disasters. Whatever this last one is, however, it will be terrible and sensational enough to catch the attention of the whole world, who will then blame God's people all over the earth and threaten them with death.

Notice that it is "the great final test." Since the calamity that precipitates the test must precede the test, obviously, the calamity must precede the close of probation by a short time. And, in fact, the test itself must precede the close of probation by a short time, since the test is what will cause all humans on earth to make their final decision for or against God. If this test were to come literally "at the close of human probation," as Ellen White said, then it could not be the test that divides the human race into two camps. Thus I understand her statement that the test will come *at* the close of probation to be "at" in a relative sense, not in the most literal sense.

---

45 White, *Testimonies for the Church*, vol. 8 (Mountain View, CA: Pacific Press Publishing Association, 1904), p. 28.
46 White, *Christ's Object Lessons*, p. 412.

Chapter 7

God Uses the Forces of Nature

One of the common themes in the Old Testament is God's intervention on behalf of His people, and His allowance of evil to discipline the wicked when they attack His people and commit all kinds of evil. These themes are particularly evident in the Psalms, Job, and the prophets, as well as in several Old Testament stories. One of the most striking features of these passages is the way God uses the forces of nature to carry out His will. He said to Job, "Have you seen the storehouses of the snow or seen the storehouses of the hail, *which I reserve* for times of trouble, *for days of war and battle*?" (Job 38:22, 23, emphasis added).

Notice that God said He uses the forces of nature as weapons for battle. This is often evident in the Psalms:

> The earth trembled and quaked, and the foundations of the mountains shook; they trembled because he was angry ... He made darkness his covering, his canopy around him—the dark rain clouds of the sky. Out of the brightness of his presence clouds advanced, with hailstones and bolts of lightning. The LORD thundered from heaven; the voice of the Most High resounded. He shot his arrows and scattered the enemy, with great bolts of lightning he routed them. The valleys of the sea were exposed and the foundations of the earth laid bare at your rebuke, LORD, at the blast of breath from your nostrils. (Ps. 18:7, 11–15)

A similar description is found in prophetic writings. Notice again that God uses the forces of nature against the wicked who are attacking Ariel (Jerusalem):

Suddenly, in an instant the LORD Almighty will come with thunder and earthquake and great noise, with windstorm and tempests and flames of devouring fire. Then the hordes of all the nations that fight against Ariel, that attack her and her fortress and besiege her, will be as it is with a dream, with a vision of the night. (Isa. 29:5–7)

Note also Luke's words: "There will be great earthquakes, famines and pestilences in various places, and fearful events and great signs from heaven" (Luke 21:11).

Since we, today, have never seen God actually use the elements in this way, it's easy for us to suppose these passages are just metaphors. However, a brief look at biblical history helps us to understand that in those moments when God has most dramatically and powerfully intervened in human affairs, He has done so through the forces of nature. In all of this, we need to remember that it is God *allowing* the disasters, and Satan *causing* them (refer to Appendix A).

Massive Destruction in Earth's History

There are at least two examples of events in earth's history in which God may have intervened with comets, asteroids, and/or meteorites. The first is Noah's flood, and the second is the destruction of Sodom and Gomorrah.

Noah's flood is an example of an intervention by God in world affairs. And how did He accomplish His purpose? Strange as it may seem, we get a clue in Genesis 2:6: "streams came up from the earth and watered the whole surface of the ground." This suggests that God created the earth with huge stores of water underground, perhaps in a vast network of caverns, the remnants of which still remain in caves such as Mammoth Cave in Kentucky and Carlsbad Caverns in New Mexico.

I have a hunch that when we reach heaven and have the opportunity to research the earth's geological history, we'll discover that a huge asteroid struck the earth at the time of the flood, shattering this vast network of underground caverns and blasting their waters onto the earth's surface. At the time of the flood, "jets of water burst forth from the earth with indescribable force, throwing massive rocks hundreds of feet into the air."[47]

Put this together with the fact that scientists tell us there's a massive asteroid impact crater, the Chicxulub Crater, fifty-two miles wide and nineteen miles deep on the Mexican Yucatan Peninsula. The asteroid itself is estimated to have been at least six miles in diameter. Evolutionary geologists estimated that the asteroid struck earth about 65 million years ago and wiped out the dinosaur population.[48]

---

47 White, *Patriarchs and Prophets* (Washington, DC: Review and Herald Publishing Association, 1890), p. 99.
48 See "Chicxulub crater," Wikipedia Foundation, last modified June 20, 2022, 15:35. https://1ref.us/7t02.

Creationists don't accept a long-earth history extending millions of years into the past, but the Chicxulub Crater certainly would be of the size required to create a massive global earthquake that could burst all the world's underground watering systems and cast huge boulders hundreds of feet into the air. Was the Chicxulub asteroid the one that set off Noah's global flood? Wait until you get to heaven and ask your attending angel about it. He should know!

Regarding the destruction of Sodom and Gomorrah, there's also evidence that it was probably caused by a meteorite impact. An article I found shows an image of a community on the shore of the Dead Sea with the caption, "Preliminary evidence indicates that a low-altitude meteor explosion around 3,700 years ago destroyed cities, villages and farmland north of the Dead Sea (shown in the background above) rendering the region uninhabitable for 600 to 700 years."[49] Interestingly, 3,700 years ago is fairly close to biblical chronology for the destruction of Sodom and Gomorrah.

Another source provides further input:

> A meteor that exploded in the air near the Dead Sea 3,700 years ago may have wiped out communities, killed tens of thousands of people, and provided the kernel of truth to an old Bible story. The area is in modern-day Jordan, in a 25 km wide circular plain called Middle Ghor. Most of the evidence for this event comes from archaeological evidence excavated at the Bronze Age city of Tall el-Hammam located in that area, which some scholars say is the city of Sodom from the Bible.[50]

Ellen White made an interesting comment about the destruction of Sodom and Gomorrah:

> As the sun arose for the last time upon the cities of the plain, the people thought to commence another day of godless riot. All were eagerly planning their business or their pleasure, and the messenger of God was derided for his fears and his warnings. Suddenly as the thunder peal from an unclouded sky, fell balls of fire on the doomed capital.[51]

---

49 Bruce Bower, "An exploding meteor may have wiped out ancient Dead Sea communities," ScienceNews, https://1ref.us/7t03.
50 Evan Gough, "A meteor may have exploded in the air 3,700 years ago, obliterating communities near the Dead Sea," Phys.org, https://1ref.us/7t04; see also https://1ref.us/7t05; https://1ref.us/7t06.
51 White, *The SDA Bible Commentary*, vol. 5 (Washington, DC: Review and Herald Publishing Association, 1956), p. 1122.

This, again, is a perfect description of a large meteor entering the earth's atmosphere, exploding, and raining down "balls of fire" that caused massive destruction. The two angels who hurried Lot and his family out of Sodom (see Gen. 19:15–17) knew exactly that about which they were talking! And the first trumpet's description of hail and fire mixed with blood falling on the earth and destroying trees and grass is not only a realistic description of meteorites striking the earth in the future; it's a realistic description of what happened to Sodom and Gomorrah several thousand years ago in the days of Abraham and Lot.

God Uses the Heavenly Bodies

Two biblical passages tell us that God uses the sun, moon, and stars to accomplish His purpose against the wicked. To get the full context, I've quoted more than just the verses that mention the heavenly bodies. I emphasized the parts relevant to the punishment of the wicked and God's use of the heavenly bodies as weapons:

> Wail, for the day of the LORD is near; it will come like a destruction from the Almighty. Because of this, all hands will go limp, every man's heart will melt. Terror will seize them, pain and anguish will grip them; they will writhe like a woman in labor. They will look aghast at each other, their faces aflame. See, the day of the LORD is coming—with wrath and fierce anger—to make the land desolate *and destroy the sinners within it.* The stars of heaven and their constellations will not show their light. *The rising sun will be darkened, and the moon will not give its light. I will punish the world for its evil, the wicked for their sins* ... Therefore I will make the heavens tremble; and the earth will shake from its place *at the wrath of the LORD Almighty, in the day of his burning anger.* (Isa. 13:6–11, 13, emphasis added)

> *The LORD is angry with all nations; his wrath is on all their armies.* He will totally destroy them, he will give them over to slaughter. Their slain will be thrown out, their dead bodies will stink; the mountains will be soaked with their blood. All the stars in the sky will be dissolved and the heavens rolled up like a scroll; *all the starry host will fall like withered leaves from the vine, like shriveled figs from the fig tree.* (Isa. 34:2–4, emphasis added)

Jesus drew on these and similar verses from the Old Testament to describe the falling of the stars and the darkening of the sun and moon, and it's to this New Testament evidence to which we will now turn.

Signs in the Heavenly Bodies in the New Testament

For 150 years, Seventh-day Adventists have said that signs in the sun, moon, and stars, exactly like those Isaiah described, would be tokens of the nearness of Christ's return. Our pioneers saw the dark day of May 19, 1780, and the falling of the stars on November 13, 1833, as fulfillments of Jesus' prophecies. However, we've believed something in the order of a dark morning in 1780 was enough to fulfill Jesus' prediction about the darkening of the sun; and we've said something in the order of a nice fireworks display over New York City on Independence Day was enough to fulfill Jesus' prediction about falling stars, for that's pretty much what happened in 1833. And to read Matthew's account, Jesus doesn't seem to have suggested much more: "Immediately after the distress of those days, 'the sun will be darkened and the moon will not give its light; the stars will fall from the sky, and the heavenly bodies will be shaken'" (Matt. 24:29).

At first glance John appears not to have suggested anything more traumatic than Jesus did: "The sun turned black like sackcloth made of goat hair, the whole moon turned blood red, and the stars in the sky fell to earth, as late figs drop from a fig tree when shaken by a strong wind" (Rev. 6:12, 13).

However, most of us haven't realized that Jesus and John were simply quoting Isaiah. And because we didn't understand this, we've also failed to recognize the full implication of the signs in the heavens that Jesus and John foretold. Isaiah included the heavenly bodies as forces of nature that God would use against the wicked, and his description goes far beyond a nice fireworks display over New York City. According to Isaiah, these signs in the heavens would be devastating calamities that would terrify those who experienced them, just as the flood terrified the antediluvians and the meteorite explosion over Sodom and Gomorrah would have terrified those residents.

A question arises: Why didn't Jesus inform us of the terrible destruction these signs in the heavenly bodies would cause? The fact is, He did. However, we've tended to quote Matthew's version in our books, articles, and sermons on the topic and generally overlooked Luke's account, but the good doctor said it plainly: "There will be signs in the sun, moon and stars.

On the earth, nations will be in anguish and perplexity at the roaring and tossing of the sea. Men will faint from terror, apprehensive of what is coming on the world, for the heavenly bodies will be shaken" (Luke 21:25, 26).

> **Why didn't Jesus inform us of the terrible destruction these signs in the heavenly bodies would cause?**

All Luke said was there would be signs in the sun, moon, and stars. He didn't say anything about dark days or falling stars. However, because Matthew *did* add these details, we can include them in our understanding of Luke's words. And notice that Luke said the nations will be "in anguish and perplexity" at these signs in the heavenly bodies. This isn't just a local reaction; it's global.

"Nations will be in anguish and perplexity." Something has to be terribly wrong in the world for its leaders to respond that dramatically to the signs in the heavens! Phenomena such as what occurred on May 19, 1780, and November 13, 1833, certainly couldn't cause it. Those events were largely observed in New England, not by the world's nations. Nevertheless, comets, asteroids, and meteorites certainly would get the world's attention!

Refer back to Luke 21:26 and notice what Jesus said: "Men will faint from terror, apprehensive of what is coming on the world, for the heavenly bodies will be shaken." It isn't just the world's government leaders who will be in anguish and perplexity; the entire human race will be in an absolute panic over the signs in the sun, moon, and stars. Again, this didn't happen in either 1780 or 1833.

There's more. Please notice what Luke said will cause the human race to be in a panic and the nations to be in anguish and perplexity: "They will be in anguish and perplexity at 'the roaring and tossing of the sea.'" I find it significant that one of the major effects of an asteroid falling into the ocean would be tidal waves, which is a perfect fit with Luke's description. An asteroid smashing into the sea would cause a massive tidal wave that would allow the flood of water to penetrate and flow hundreds of miles into any nearby coastal area. Ellen White supported this conclusion:

> "And there shall be signs in the sun, and in the moon, and in the stars; and upon the earth distress of nations, with perplexity; the sea and the waves roaring" (Luke 21:25). Yes, they shall pass their

borders, and destruction will be in their track. They will engulf the ships that sail upon their broad waters, and with the burden of their living freight, they will be hurried into eternity, without time to repent.[52]

Please note that in the context of the signs in the sun, moon, and stars, White said the sea and waves will pass their borders. The technical term for the seas passing their borders is "tsunami," also known as "tidal wave," and, as we've already seen, of the heavenly signs—sun, moon, and stars—only the falling of the stars (i.e., an asteroid) could cause a tidal wave. In addition, it is well-established that earthquakes can also result in tsunamis.

Finally, I will call your attention to Jesus' statement: "Then there will be great distress, unequaled from the beginning of the world until now—and never to be equaled again. If those days had not been cut short, no one would survive, but for the sake of the elect, those days will be shortened" (Matt. 24:21, 22). When He said these words, Jesus clearly had in mind Daniel's prediction that at the very end of time, "there will be a time of distress such as has not happened from the beginning of nations until then" (Dan. 12:1).

However, Jesus added to Daniel's words. He said, "If those days had not been cut short, *no one would survive*" (emphasis added). Consider Jesus' prediction in its most literal sense. He said if God should allow the distress of the last days to continue unabated, the human race would become the next extinct species. That's what "no one would survive" means. And scientists tell us the impact of a major asteroid, or a series of smaller ones, could very easily wipe out the human race. Is it any wonder that the nations will be in anguish and perplexity and the human race will be terrified at the signs in the heavenly bodies?

In view of the fact that the first four trumpets are such an accurate description of the effects of comets, asteroids, and meteorites striking our earth, I have no trouble believing they are simply a more detailed account than the one Jesus gave of the falling of the stars and the fallout from that. For those who disagree with my interpretation of the trumpets, Jesus' words are enough to make the point, for primarily comets, asteroids, and meteorites could cause the tidal waves and global terror He foretold. These calamities from the heavenly bodies would threaten the survival of the human race. And Ellen White's description of the end-time judgments of

---

52   White, *Selected Messages*, book 3, p. 417.

God that we saw in the previous chapter are clearly of a magnitude that comets, asteroids, and meteorites could very easily cause.

There can be no doubt that in the very near future, the world will experience natural disasters far more horrible than anything it has ever seen in recorded history.

Chapter 8

The First Four Trumpets

We are now ready to begin examining the trumpets themselves, and this is a challenge because they have puzzled many Seventh-day Adventists interpreters of apocalyptic prophecy for 175 years. In chapter 2, I quoted Jon Paulien. To reiterate, the first four trumpets are "one of the most difficult passages in the Apocalypse."[53] Additionally, he said, "if you asked twelve students of Revelation what the seven trumpets are all about, you'd probably get at least thirteen different opinions."[54]

Why is this? What makes the seven trumpets so much more of a challenge to interpret compared to the rest of Revelation? I will make a suggestion: With respect to the first four trumpets, we've tried to interpret them symbolically when they need to be understood literally. The problem with a symbolic interpretation is that there are no clues in either of the Bible's apocalyptic books, Daniel and Revelation, to aid us in the symbolic interpretation of the first four trumpets. I will explain what I mean by reviewing with you three examples of symbols that *are* explained in either book.

Take the case of the two beast powers in Revelation 13. We know from Daniel 7 that a beast in apocalyptic prophecy represents a political entity—a nation or kingdom. This is obvious from the explanation the angel gave to Daniel: "The four great beasts are four kingdoms that will rise from the earth" (Dan. 7:17). Therefore, it only makes sense that the beasts that rise from the sea and the land in Revelation 13 should also represent political entities.

We also know that a body of water such as a sea represents people—a populated area of the world—because John's angel interpreter told him "the waters you saw, where the prostitute sits, are peoples, multitudes, nations, and languages" (Rev. 17:15). Therefore, it makes sense to understand that the beast that rises from the sea in Revelation 13:1 comes from a populated part of the world, while the beast that rises up from the land in verse 11 comes from a relatively unpopulated part of the world.

---

53 Paulien, *Decoding Revelation's Trumpets: Literary Allusions and Interpretations of Revelation 8:7–12*, p. 421.
54 Paulien, *Seven Keys: Unlocking the Secrets of Revelation* (Nampa, Idaho: Pacific Press Publishing Association, 2009), p. 83.

Then there's the fact that much of the symbolism in Revelation 13 arises from the apocalyptic prophecy of Daniel 7, especially verse 25. For example, the beast from the sea blasphemes God (see Rev. 13:5) the same way Daniel's little horn blasphemed God (see Dan. 7:25). The sea beast in Revelation 13 "make[s] war against the saints and ... conquer[s] them" (Rev. 13:7) the same way Daniel's little horn oppresses God's saints. And the beast from the sea "exercise[s] his authority for forty-two months" (Rev. 13:5) the same way Daniel's little horn is given authority over the saints "for a time, times, and half a time" (see Dan. 7:25).

Nevertheless, coming back to Revelation 8:7–12, there are no such aids for interpreting the trumpets. Traditionally, Adventist interpreters have compared the various words and ideas in the first four trumpets with similar words and concepts in the Old Testament, especially their occurrence in the classical prophets. And then we try to make these words in the first four trumpets fit the history of nations during the 2,000 years of Christian history. It's no wonder nearly all these students of prophecy make cautious statements like the ones I pointed out in chapter 2! They *assume* their interpretation is what the prophet meant; their interpretation *may be regarded as* the meaning of the prophecy; or the symbol *seems to portray* the meaning the interpreter is giving it. It's no wonder that for every twelve interpreters of the trumpets, there are at least thirteen interpretations!

As I suggested earlier in this chapter, the reason why we've had so much difficulty interpreting the first four trumpets during our 175-year history is that we are trying to interpret them symbolically when, in fact, they need to be understood literally. I know this will be difficult for many of my fellow students of the trumpets to accept, but I ask you to hear me out. I will begin with the first four trumpets, which go together as a group:

> Then the seven angels who had the seven trumpets prepared to sound them. The first angel sounded his trumpet, and there came hail and fire mixed with blood, and it was hurled down upon the earth. A third of the earth was burned up, a third of the trees were burned up, and all the green grass was burned up. The second angel sounded his trumpet, and something like a huge mountain, all ablaze, was thrown into the sea. A third of the sea turned into blood, a third of the living creatures in the sea died, and a third of the ships were destroyed. The third angel sounded his trumpet, and a great star, blazing like a torch, fell from the sky on a third of the rivers and on the springs of water—the name of the star is Wormwood. A third

of the waters turned bitter, and many people died from the waters that had become bitter. The fourth angel sounded his trumpet, and a third of the sun was struck, a third of the moon, and a third of the stars, so that a third of them turned dark. A third of the day was without light, and also a third of the night. (Rev. 8:6–12)

I repeat that the first issue we need to settle as we attempt to interpret these four trumpet blasts is whether they should be understood literally or symbolically. In the first chapter of this book, I pointed out that a basic principle of Seventh-day Adventist prophetic interpretation is that an apocalyptic prophecy should be interpreted literally unless it is clearly symbolic. Adventists have traditionally favored a symbolic interpretation of the first four trumpets because a literal interpretation seemed impossible. Our pioneers would have laughed at the idea that hail and fire could literally fall from the sky, and even if it did, how could it burn up a third of the earth, a third of the trees, and all the green grass? How, they would have asked, could a mountain ever fall out of the sky into the ocean, turn a third of its water into blood, kill a third of its fish, and destroy a third of the ships? The principle that apocalyptic prophecy is to be interpreted symbolically unless it can have a clear, literal interpretation compelled our pioneers to interpret the first four trumpets symbolically because they had no reasonable basis for a literal interpretation.

However, today, a literal interpretation makes perfectly good sense, as we shall see. I will begin by sharing with you a closer look at the first four trumpets in the chart below:

Trumpet	Agent	Result
First	Hail and fire mixed with blood is hurled upon the earth.	A third of the earth, a third of the trees, and all the green grass are burned up.
Second	A huge mountain, all ablaze, is cast into the sea.	A third of the sea turns to blood, a third of the living creatures die, and a third of the ships are destroyed.
Third	A blazing star falls on the sea and the fountains of water.	The fresh water supplies turn bitter, and many people die.
Fourth	None	A third of the sun, moon, and stars turn dark.

If you look carefully at the "Result" column above, you'll see the first four trumpets, when understood literally, describe terrible *ecological* disasters. Furthermore, these disasters affect the earth's environment in the very ways about which the human race is so profoundly concerned. We're legitimately worried about the pollution of the earth and its forests, the sea, the sources of fresh water, and the atmosphere.

> *These disasters will be a clear signal to the world that God has intervened in human affairs.*

One might conclude that the first trumpet is acid rain falling on the trees and the pesticides leaching into the earth. The second trumpet could be chemical pollution of our lakes and seas; the third trumpet might be chemical and radioactive pollution of our fresh water supplies from industrial and nuclear wastes buried in the earth; and the fourth trumpet may be pollution of our atmosphere by smoke from factories and the exhaust from motor vehicles, commercial jets, etc.

That's an attractive theory, but it makes the source of these disasters human neglect, not judgments from God. According to Revelation, these disasters will come upon the earth at God's initiative, not ours. They will be a clear signal to the world that He has intervened in human affairs. Nobody would ever get that idea from ecological disasters that are obviously the result of our own human negligence.

The Cause of the First Four Trumpets

If the first four trumpets are ecological devastation, the next question we must ask is, What causes this destruction? The best way to answer that question is to look at what the prophecy itself says about the cause:

First trumpet: "Hail and fire mixed with blood *was hurled down upon the earth.*" **Second trumpet:** "Something like a huge mountain, all ablaze, *was thrown into the sea.*" **Third trumpet:** "A great star, blazing like a torch, *fell from the sky* on a third of the rivers and on the springs of water."

Fourth trumpet: No cause is mentioned, only the result.

Notice that when we examine the agents in the first three trumpets that cause ecological devastation, we discover that in each case, the agent falls on the world, either onto the land, sea, or water sources. From where do these objects come? The third trumpet is the only one that explains the origin of these objects: the sky. However, all three of them fell from *above* the world *onto* the world, which means they came from the sky. If the first four trumpets discuss literal ecological disasters that are coming upon the world and the cause will literally be fiery objects falling from the sky, then I can think of only one possibility: comets, asteroids, or meteorites.

As recently as 1975, I could not have written what I'm going to tell you next without seeming utterly foolish to any scientist worth his or her weight in salt, for only since about 1980 has the scientific community taken seriously the idea that comets, asteroids, and meteorites have caused major damage to our earth in the past. In 1980, when the hypothesis that asteroids might have had a major influence on earth's geological history was first suggested, it was accepted by only a few scientists. Most ridiculed the idea. However, today the majority of scientists recognize that asteroid impacts on the earth have indeed been the cause of unimaginable geological change and environmental devastation. They also recognize that these disasters will almost certainly happen again someday, though they obviously cannot predict exactly when.[55]

A number of years ago, I asked a friend who is a Seventh-day Adventist geologist to give me his opinion about the first four trumpets in light of current scientific thought regarding asteroid impacts. I handed him my Bible and pointed to Revelation 8:6–12. I felt apprehensive as he read, certain he would hand the Bible back with a condescending smile and suggest I look elsewhere for my interpretation of the passage. I wasn't prepared for his response. He said, "These four trumpets describe perfectly the ecological devastation that scientists know would be caused by a major asteroid impact on the earth or in the ocean."

My study of this subject since that time has persuaded me to conclude that my geologist friend was absolutely correct. Many reliable sources are available today that describe the probable effect[56] of a major asteroid

---

55 "'Earth runs its course about the sun in a swarm of asteroids,' says astronomer Yeomans of NASA's Jet Propulsion Laboratory in Pasadena, California. 'Sooner or later, our planet will be struck by one of them'" (*Newsweek*, November 23, 1992, pp. 56, 57).

56 Notice I said, "Many reliable sources are available today that describe the *probable effect* of a major asteroid impact." Nobody in recent history has observed a major asteroid impact on either the land or sea, so scientists have to rely on what we *do* know and what we *can* observe to estimate the *probable* effect of an asteroid impact.

impact, a number of which have been written in language the average person can understand. In the rest of this chapter, I will share with you what I've learned.

Comets, Asteroids, and Meteorites

Comets are quite different from asteroids and meteorites, but the latter two differ only in their size. Meteorites measure up to a few feet across. An asteroid is any object from outer space that measures a few yards to several miles in diameter. A quarter-mile asteroid would devastate the region where it struck and could have profound consequences on the ecology of the entire planet. An asteroid several miles in diameter would leave a crater fifty or more miles across and devastate the entire world. In the previous chapter, I mentioned the massive Chicxulub crater, partly on Mexico's Yucatan Peninsula and partly in the Caribbean Sea, that was caused by a massive asteroid estimated to have been six miles across. On the next several pages, I will describe for you what scientists have determined was the probable effect this asteroid had on the world and compare that with what the Bible says about the effect of the first four trumpets. I'll begin with the following statement:[57]

> The scenario is straight out of a science fiction movie: Giant meteorite strikes earth, setting the planet afire. Volcanoes erupt, tsunamis crash into continents. The sky grows dark for months, perhaps years. Unable to cope with the catastrophic changes in climate, countless species are wiped off the face of the planet.
>
> Yet this is the apocalyptic scene scientists suggest, as evidence grows that comets or meteorites may indeed be the agents of mass destruction on earth.[58]

Let's find out what my geologist friend meant when he said the first four trumpets "describe perfectly the ecological devastation that we know would be caused by a major asteroid impact on the earth." Most of the quotations below describe the worldwide devastation that would be caused by an asteroid six miles across. The devastation caused by the first four

---

57 I mentioned in the introduction to this manuscript that I began my research on the relationship between comets, asteroids, and meteorites on the one hand and the first four trumpets on the other back around 1990. Some of the scientific evidence I will share with you on the next few pages come from those sources, and some are from more recent research I did thirty years later, in 2020.
58 Rick Gore, "Extinctions," *National Geographic*, June 1989, p. 686.

trumpets is much more limited—only a third of the sea, trees, etc. are affected. If the first four trumpets indeed describe future meteorite, asteroid, and perhaps comet impacts on the earth, as I have suggested, these astronomical bodies would have to be smaller than six miles in diameter.

The First Trumpet

John described the first trumpet as "hail and fire mixed with blood" falling on the earth. That sounds strange. How could hail, fire, and blood fall on the earth in any literal sense? Quite easily, actually, though it would not be real blood of course, and the hail wouldn't necessarily be made out of ice. Let's examine the evidence.

Hail. There are two possibilities for the hail. It could be a shower of meteorites or the pieces of a broken-up comet. The idea that it might be a meteorite shower is not difficult for Adventists to understand. We are, after all, very familiar with the meteorite shower that occurred on November 13, 1833. The primary difference between that event and what the first trumpet predicts is that the meteorites in 1833 were viewed in the sky, whereas the meteorites foretold by the first trumpet will strike the earth or perhaps explode in midair before they hit the planet. The idea that the hail in the first trumpet might be the pieces of a broken-up comet seems more farfetched, but evidence does exist to support that conclusion. A journal of the National Space Society[59] published an article that included the following statement:

> [Asteroid expert Eugene] Shoemaker believes, "a sun-grazing comet … a few tens of kilometers across broke up during a near pass by the sun and made a compact stream of debris." In other words, a giant shotgun shell of cometary debris played Russian roulette with Earth.[60]

This would fit the first trumpet's description of hail falling to the earth and burning up the grass and trees.

Fire. The fire associated with the hail in John's vision is easy enough to understand. We've all seen the fiery streaks made by shooting stars. Large meteorites would create huge fireballs.

---

59 The National Space Society includes many respected astronomers and space scientists in its membership.
60 John Kross, "Hitting Home," *Ad Astra*, November/December 1992, p. 31.

Blood. We should understand the "blood" John saw to be some red substance, not actual blood. And it's now well known that meteors, as they plunge through the atmosphere toward earth, give off a variety of colors, depending on the composition of the meteor.

> The color of many Leonids[61] is caused by light emitted from metal atoms from the meteoroid (blue, green, and yellow) and light emitted by atoms and molecules of the air (red). The metal atoms emit light much like in our sodium discharge lamps: sodium (Na) atoms give an orange-yellow light, iron (Fe) atoms a yellow light, magnesium (Mg) a blue- green light, ionized calcium (Ca+) atoms may add a violet hue, while molecules of atmospheric nitrogen (N2) and oxygen atoms (O) *give a red light.* The meteor color depends on whether the metal atom emissions or the air plasma emissions dominate.[62]

Thus, John's description of "hail and fire mixed with blood" fits what we today know about the possible effect of a meteorite shower. It *can* look blood red.

Here is Nate Gore's description of a meteorite impact on the earth:

> As much as 90 percent of the world's forests must have burned … The fireball would have had a radius of several thousand kilometers. Winds of hundreds of kilometers an hour would have swept the planet for hours, drying trees like a giant hair dryer. Two-thousand-degree rock vapor would have spread rapidly. It would have condensed to white-hot grains that could have started additional fires.
>
> In addition, lightning discharges like those in a volcanic eruption could have ignited windswept fires on all landmasses.[63]

Of course, an asteroid that burned up 90 percent of the world's forests would be much larger than would be the meteorites described by the first trumpet, which Revelation said would destroy only a third of the world's forests. Therefore, let's look at a much smaller event that has happened in fairly recent human history. I'm referring to a massive explosion that occurred in an unpopulated part of the Siberian forests on June 30, 1908. Named after the Tunguska River, where it happened, it destroyed 830

---

61   A Leonid is a shower of meteors that occurs around mid-November each year and appears to radiate from a point in the constellation Leo.
62   "Background facts on meteors and meteor showers," NASA, https://1ref.us/7t07 (emphasis added).
63   Gore, "Extinctions," *National Geographic*, June 1989, p. 673.

square miles of forest. The cause was probably a small comet or asteroid,[64] which, since it left no impact crater, most likely burst about three to six miles above ground. It flattened an estimated 80 million trees within those 830 square miles. Estimates made by scientists who have studied the area in the years since 1908 suggest the asteroid was somewhere between 160 and 200 feet in diameter.[65]

"Oh, but the hail of the first trumpet will supposedly destroy a third of the earth's forest, not 830 square miles," you may say. True, but keep in mind it is *hail,* and hail is many balls of ice or, in this case, meteors. Therefore, multiply the Tunguska event by 100 or 1,000 meteors, each at 160–200 feet in diameter, all plunging to earth at the same time—because that's what hail does. Suddenly, the blood red becomes visible to our imaginations, and the massive destruction of forests becomes very realistic. And keep in mind that today's scientists know an event of this sort *is* possible. It *literally* could happen.

The Second Trumpet

The second trumpet looked to John like a mountain all ablaze that fell into the sea. A "mountain" can be anywhere from a half mile to several miles across, so this would clearly be an asteroid. Of special significance, however, is the devastation it would cause, which is entirely consistent with what scientists predict would happen if an asteroid were to crash in the ocean. John said, "a third of the sea turned into blood, [and] a third of the living creatures in the sea died" (Rev. 8:8, 9). The explanation for the sea turning to blood and killing the living creatures is called "red tide."

Red tide is a phenomenon that occurs fairly frequently off both the Eastern and Western coasts of the United States. It's caused by a red organism so tiny that it can be seen only under magnification. Huge masses of these organisms can turn the ocean blood-red, and their presence in the water kills any living creature that's unfortunate enough to live in that habitat. Most significant for our purpose is the condition that causes red tide. Here's some insight regarding the result of a six-mile asteroid's impact on the oceans:

---

64 An analysis of microscopic particles from near the center of the impact suggest it was a meteorite or small asteroid.
65 See "Tunguska event," Wikipedia Foundation, last modified June 18, 2022, 14:24. https://1ref.us/7t08.

In a new study, researchers simulated how the spherules of molten and vaporized rock ejected from the impact would have behaved as they were sent into the atmosphere and fell back down to earth. Upon re-entry these tiny fireballs created large amounts of the gases nitric oxide and nitrogen dioxide—known collectively as nitrogen oxides.

The study suggests these gases came back down to Earth as acid rain and increased the nitrate levels in the oceans, stimulating a massive global algal bloom [the scientific name for "red tide"]. This algal bloom could have generated harmful toxins and disrupted the marine ecosystem, potentially triggering the massive die-off that followed the extinction of the dinosaurs, according to the study's authors.[66]

I also found the following information about red tide: "Harmful algal blooms, or HABs, occur when colonies of algae ... grow out of control ... produc[ing] powerful toxins that can kill fish, shellfish, mammals, and birds."[67] Therefore, John's description of the sea turning blood-red fits perfectly with what scientists know an asteroid crashing into the ocean would do.

John also said the second trumpet would destroy one-third of the ships in the sea. Again, this is entirely realistic. "If the [six-mile asteroid] ... hit in the Gulf of Mexico, it would have created a wave three miles [16,000 feet] high. Nine hundred miles away, the mammoth wall of water would still be 1,500 feet high. Such an asteroid ... would cause floods in Kansas City."[68]

A tidal wave of that magnitude, or even one caused by a much smaller asteroid, would destroy any ship that was unfortunate enough to get in its path. Even a quarter-mile asteroid would create a tidal wave hundreds of feet high—large enough to destroy ships and obliterate any coastal area over which it washed.[69]

In a statement I quoted in a previous chapter, Ellen White said, "O that God's people had a sense of the impending destruction of thousands of cities, now almost given to idolatry."[70] Now read the following quotations:

> When the monster [a six-mile asteroid] made contact with the ocean bed, 100 million megatons of energy would be released, eventually

---

66   Lillian Steenblik Hwang, "Dinosaur-killing asteroid may have caused global algal bloom, marine extinction," American Geophysical Union, December 4, 2015. https://1ref.us/7t09.
67   "What is a red tide?" National Oceanic and Atmospheric Administration. https://1ref.us/7t10.
68   Sharon Begley, "The Science of Doom," Newsweek, November 23, 1992, p. 60.
69   Comets, Asteroids, and Meteorites (Alexandria, Virginia: Time-Life Books, 1992), p. 52.
70   White, Evangelism, p. 29.

shaking the entire planet ... In the passage of only three minutes, an expanding fireball of steam and molten ejecta would level any city within a distance of 1,200 miles and scour the terrain down to bedrock.[71]

The Third Trumpet

John described the third trumpet as "a great star, blazing like a torch" that fell from the sky "onto a third of the rivers and on the springs of water" (Rev. 8:10). The name of the star is "Wormwood," which means "bitter," and it pollutes a large part of the world's fresh water supplies. Many people die from the poisoned water, presumably from drinking it.

What is this third trumpet? From John's description, it could be either a comet or asteroid. The question is, How could an asteroid pollute the world's fresh water supply? Again, this is entirely consistent with what is known about an asteroid striking the earth:

> The toxic rainfall [resulting from an asteroid impact] would defoliate any remaining land plants, acidify lakes, and leach normally insoluble, highly poisonous metals from soils and rocks, depositing them in streams, ponds, and rivers, where they would sicken or kill much of the surviving aquatic life.[72]

The Fourth Trumpet

The Bible doesn't mention the cause of the darkening of the heavenly bodies under the fourth trumpet. However, if what I've said about the first three trumpets is true, then the cause of this darkening of the sun is clear: The first and third asteroids striking the earth would cast massive quantities of dust into the upper atmosphere, and the jet stream would scatter this dust all over the world within just one day. Notice the following quotation, again describing the effect of an asteroid six miles in diameter:

> Trillions of tons of microfine rock particles and condensed vapor droplets thrown up by the asteroid impact would soar spaceward, reaching stratospheric heights within seconds ...

---

71   *Comets, Asteroids, and Meteorites*, p. 127.
72   *Ibid.*, p. 133.

Soot from the fires mixed with nitrogen oxide smog produced by the initial and subsequent shock waves would combine with the rapidly spreading dust to form a cloud seventeen miles thick. It would envelop the entire world within twenty-four hours … The surface of the earth would be locked away in a blackness thirty times more inky than the darkest moonless night.[73]

The fourth trumpet describes only a partial darkening of the sun, moon, and stars. Thus, the asteroid causing the darkness would have to be much smaller than six miles in diameter.

Conclusion

My geologist friend was right. The global ecological devastation described in the first four trumpets is entirely consistent with what modern science knows about the effects of comets, asteroids, and meteorites striking the earth. If we apply the principle that an apocalyptic prophecy is to be understood literally unless a literal interpretation would be impossible, then I believe scientific thought as it has developed since 1980 makes it entirely reasonable to understand the first four trumpets literally. And if this part of Revelation is indeed literal, then the consequences for our planet's future are truly awesome.

> *I believe scientific thought makes it entirely reasonable to understand the first four trumpets literally.*

I will mention one other conclusion I believe is entirely realistic in light of what I've shared with you in this chapter. Have you ever noticed the first three gospels, Matthew, Mark, and Luke, all mention Jesus' prediction about the falling stars and the darkening of the sun and moon as signs of the end, but John's gospel is totally silent on this point? Perhaps one reason for this omission is that John included the falling of the stars in his apocalypse: once in his description of the sixth seal (see Rev. 6:12, 13), and again in the passage on the first four trumpets. I believe the first four trumpets are the same thing as the falling of the stars and the darkening of the sun and moon in the first three gospels.

---

73 *Ibid.*, p. 131.

The similarity between the signs in the sun, moon, and stars in Luke's gospel and that in the first four trumpets is especially evident in Luke's account. He said that as a result of the signs in the sun, moon, and stars, "nations will be in anguish and perplexity at the roaring and tossing of the sea" (Luke 21:25). The falling of the stars in 1833 didn't come close to creating international panic, or cause a tidal wave anywhere in the world. However, that's exactly what an asteroid striking one of earth's oceans would do. And keep in mind that an asteroid *is* a falling star.

Chapter 9

Aftermath of the First Four Trumpets

When the angel in Revelation 8:2–5 casts down his censer, probation for the world will close, and God will remove His protection from earth. This will open the way for the trumpets to begin sounding. This will also be the time when the four angels in Revelation 7:1–3 are allowed to release the four winds they had been holding. Then the world will be plunged into an environmental crisis such as has not been seen since the time of Noah's flood. Thus will begin the fulfillment of Daniel's prediction that at the time of the end, Michael will stand up, and "there will be a time of distress such as has not happened from the beginning of nations until then" (Dan. 12:1). This will also begin the fulfillment of Jesus' statement regarding the end time that there is coming a time of "great distress, unequaled from the beginning of the world until now—and never to be equaled again" (Matt. 24:21).

Small areas of the world have experienced devastation of this magnitude, but never has the whole world experienced this. When a terrible natural disaster such as a hurricane or earthquake occurs somewhere in the world, we are accustomed to seeing relief agencies rush in with help. In the United States, the president usually proclaims the region a disaster area, and the federal government provides additional support.

However, two things will be different about the coming season of calamity. First, the devastation will be so widespread and over such a vast region that relief sufficient to cover all the needs will be impossible to provide. Second, and far more significant, will be the devastating consequences of the disaster to the world's ecology. Think of what Jesus said: "The sun will be darkened and the moon will not give its light" (Matt. 24:29). If the cause of this phenomenon is the falling of the stars, which Jesus also mentioned in this verse, then the darkening of the sun and moon will be easily explainable. As I pointed out in the previous chapter, an asteroid even a quarter mile in diameter striking the earth would cast millions of tons of dust into the upper atmosphere. It would set fire to thousands of square miles of any nearby forests, and within twenty-four hours, a shroud of dust and smoke would envelop the globe, possibly causing a mild ice age.

The world's scientists are already concerned about the damage to the environment that has been caused by 200 years of technological development. They are already concerned about smog, acid rain, and the pollution of our rivers and streams by chemicals, pesticides, and plain old garbage. What will the world's politicians do? What will the world's religious leaders do? The response that scientists, politicians, and religious leaders are giving today to the environmental crisis gives us clue. It was already beginning back in the early 1990s:

> In Washington, D.C. this May [1991], a unique gathering will take place. Leaders of many of the major religions in America will meet with scientists from many fields, and the two groups [will set aside] ancient differences ... for the common good. The focus: To help preserve the planetary environment on which our mutual well-being depends.
>
> It's a heady vision—scientists and religious leaders (and a growing number of politicians) teaming up to explain their concerns about the worsening environmental crisis and to urge changes in the way our species conducts itself.[74]

Carl Sagan, the scientist who wrote the words above, is a confirmed secular humanist. Yet notice the religious overtone to his article:

> There is a clear theme [in all religions] that the natural world is a creation of God, put here for purposes separate from the glorification of "Man" and deserving, therefore, of respect and care in its own right, not just because of its utility for us. A poignant metaphor of "stewardship" has emerged, especially recently—the idea that humans are the caretakers of the Earth, put here for the purpose and accountable, now and into the indefinite future, to the Landlord.[75]

Especially significant is the grand ecumenical overtone to the meeting about which Sagan tells us:

> Nearly 100 nations were present at the "Global Forum of Spiritual and Parliamentary Leaders" meetings at Oxford April 1988 and in

---

74 Carl Sagan, article title unknown, *Parade*, March 1991.
75 *Ibid.*

Moscow in 1990. Standing under an immense photograph of Earth from space, I found myself looking out over a diversely costumed representation of the wondrous variety of our species: Mother Teresa and the Cardinal Archbishop of Vienna, the Archbishop of Canterbury, the chief rabbis of Romania and the United Kingdom, the Grand Mufti of Syria, the high priest of the sacred forest of Togo, the Dalai Lama, Jain priests resplendent in their white robes, turbaned Sikhs, Hindu Swamis, Buddhist abbots, Shinto priests, evangelical Protestants, the Primate of the Armenian Church, a "living Buddha" from China, the bishops of Stockholm and Harare, metropolitans of the Orthodox Churches, the Chief of Chiefs of the Six Nations of the Iroquois Confederacy—and joining them, the secretary-general of the United Nations; the prime minister of Norway; the founder of a Kenyan women's movement to replant forests; the president of World Watch Institute; the directors of the United Nations Children's Fund, its Population fund and UNESCO; the Soviet minister of the environment; and parliamentarians from dozens of nations, including U.S. Senators and Representatives.[76]

Then there's the Paris Climate Agreement, which resulted from a convention of representatives from 196 of the world's nations that met near Paris in December 2015. Under the agreement, each of the signatory nations was supposed to take action to reduce its emissions of greenhouse gases in order to keep the global rise in temperature to no more than 1.5 degrees centigrade above preindustrial levels.[77]

However, what's most significant for our purposes in this chapter is the fact that the Paris Climate Agreement (or Accord) would almost certainly not have been voted—nor would the meeting itself in all likelihood have even been held—had it not been for the pressure put on the nations by Pope Francis. Francis is using the issue of climate change as a major tool to increase the Vatican's influence over global politics. And one can only imagine the impact comets, asteroids, and meteorites devastating our planet under the four trumpets will have on the papacy's global influence. If the world's scientists, politicians, and religious leaders are getting together *now* to resolve *today's* environmental crisis, what will they do then, when the real crisis is upon us?

---

76 *Ibid.*
77 See "Paris Agreement," Wikipedia Foundation, last modified June 7, 2022, 16:19. https://1ref.us/249.

Norman Schwarzkopf, the American general who commanded the coalition of forces against Saudi Arabia during Operation Desert Storm, suggested something that gives us an interesting clue:

> Germany should stop hiding behind its constitution and get involved in military operations like the gulf war or the U.S.-led mission in Somalia ....
>
> Schwarzkopf was quoted in Tuesday's issue of *Stern* magazine as saying the constitution gives Germans "a wonderful excuse to say, 'I can't get involved because my constitution prevents it.'"
>
> *Stern* quoted him as saying, "Constitutions can be changed. And as the world situation changes, constitutions, in my mind, should be changed."[78]

"As the world changes, constitutions ... should be changed." That's a sobering thought, particularly when we follow it up with a statement made more than 100 years ago about a change in the United States Constitution:

> By the decree enforcing the institution of the papacy in violation of the law of God, our nation will disconnect herself fully from righteousness. When Protestantism shall stretch her hand across the gulf to grasp the hand of the Roman power, when she shall reach over the abyss to clasp hands with spiritualism, when, under the influence of this threefold union, *our country shall repudiate every principle of its Constitution* as a Protestant and republican government, and shall make provision for the propagation of papal falsehoods and delusions, then we may know that the time has come for the marvelous working of Satan and that the end is near.
>
> As the approach of the Roman armies was a sign to the disciples of the impending destruction of Jerusalem, so may this apostasy be a sign to us that the limit of God's forbearance is reached, that the measure of our nation's iniquity is full, and that the angel of mercy is about to take her flight, never to return.[79]

It's important, I believe, that we understand clearly what Schwarzkopf and Ellen White are *not* saying. Schwarzkopf is not talking about changing constitutions in order to persecute people; he is not talking about changing constitutions in order to make Roman Catholic doctrine the law of the

---

78 "Germany Urged to Act with Military," *Tampa Bay Times*, December 16, 1992.
79 White, *Testimonies for the Church*, vol. 5, p. 451 (emphasis added).

land; and he certainly is not talking about changing constitutions in order to make way for Sunday laws.

Notice, also, that Ellen White did not say the United States Constitution will be *changed*. She said its principles will be *repudiated*. This can happen through an act of Congress or reinterpretation by the Supreme Court, neither of which is changing the Constitution but both of which are repudiating its principles.

Now that we've paid careful attention to what Schwarzkopf and Ellen White did *not* say, let's look at their words in light of what we've learned so far in this book about how the final crisis might develop:

When ...

- the world's ecology has been shattered
- the majority of the world's grain crops have been destroyed (see Rev. 8:7)
- thousands of cities lie in ruins from fire and flood (see *Evangelism*, p. 29)
- millions around the world are injured and dying
- the whole world is threatened with starvation
- the world's nations are in anguish and perplexity and the human race is in terror over the crisis (see Luke 21:25, 26)
- demons in the guise of beings purportedly from another galaxy offer to help us solve the crisis

Then ...

- the world's political, religious, and scientific leaders, along with the "beings from another galaxy," will get together to solve the crisis
- one solution could be to change the constitutions of the world's nations
- the solution suggested will include both practical help and recommendations for spiritual commitment
- a poll taken at that time would show the whole world was in agreement that, given the seriousness of the situation, the solution the world's leaders and the "beings from another galaxy" came up with was appropriate
- drastic action, such as that predicted in Revelation 13, will seem just as sensible as did the American intervention in Afghanistan and Syria

- those who refuse to go along with the plan will be accused of disaffection toward the government

I'm convinced by the inspired evidence that something like this *will* happen someday as a result of the terrible judgments we know are coming upon the world.

Chapter 10

The Fifth Trumpet

As terrible as the first four trumpets are (or will be), John introduced the last three trumpets with these awesome words: "As I watched, I heard an eagle that was flying in midair call out in a loud voice: 'Woe! Woe! Woe to the inhabitants of the earth, because of the trumpet blasts about to be sounded by the other three angels'" (Rev. 8:13).

Obviously, no literal eagle[80] will ever call out such a message from the sky. This eagle must be understood symbolically. John's eagle seems to be saying to the world, "If you thought the first four trumpets were bad, wait 'til you see the last three!"

> The fifth angel sounded his trumpet, and I saw a star that had fallen from the sky to the earth. The star was given the key to the shaft of the Abyss. When he opened the Abyss, smoke rose from it like the smoke from a gigantic furnace. The sun and sky were darkened by the smoke from the Abyss. And out of the smoke locusts came down on the earth and were given power like that of scorpions of the earth. They were told not to harm the grass of the earth or any plant or tree, but only those people who did not have the seal of God on their foreheads. They were not allowed to kill them but only to torture them for five months. And the agony they suffered was like that of the sting of a scorpion when it strikes. During those days people will seek death but will not find it; they will long to die, but death will elude them. The locusts looked like horses prepared for battle. On their heads they wore something like crowns of gold, and their faces resembled human faces. Their hair was like women's hair, and their teeth were like lions' teeth. They had breastplates like breastplates of iron, and the sound of their wings was like the thundering of many horses and chariots rushing into battle. They had tails with stingers, like scorpions, and in their tails they had power

---

80 The King James Version says "angel." *The Seventh-day Adventist Bible Commentary* says, "textual evidence favors ... the reading 'an eagle.' The eagle may be thought of as an omen of doom (see Matt. 24:28; cf. Deut. 28:49; Hosea 8:1; Hab. 1:8)."

to torment people for five months. They had as king over them the angel of the Abyss, whose name in Hebrew is Abaddon and in Greek is Apollyon. (Rev. 9:1–11)

As we examine the fifth trumpet, there are several issues at which we need to look: the star that falls from the sky, the locusts the star releases from the Abyss, and the Abyss itself. Are these literal or symbolic? And if they are symbolic, what do they represent? These are the questions to which we will be seeking answers.

The Star That Had Fallen from the Sky

In Revelation 9:1, John saw a star that had fallen from heaven, and the star was given the key to the Abyss (KJV, "bottomless pit"). Should we understand this star literally or symbolically? This question is particularly relevant in view of the fact that I have interpreted a star and other objects falling from the sky in the first four trumpets literally. Are there any reasons for interpreting the star in the fifth trumpet symbolically? Quite a few, actually. Remember the principle I stated in chapter 1 that we should interpret the details of an apocalyptic prophecy literally unless a literal interpretation would clearly be impossible. I think it's fairly obvious that a literal interpretation of the star in the fifth trumpet is impossible because Revelation's description of the star treats it as though it were intelligent. It's given the key to the Abyss, and in verse 2, we learn the star opens the Abyss. Stars can't literally do that. That's why I conclude the star in the fifth trumpet must be understood symbolically. With that said, what is it?

> **Are there any reasons for interpreting the star in the fifth trumpet symbolically? Quite a few, actually.**

It's fairly common knowledge among Adventist interpreters of apocalyptic prophecy that a star represents one of God's angels or people, and a fallen star represents a fallen person or angel.[81] For the following reasons, I believe this star represents Satan:

- John didn't see this star fall. He said at the time the fifth trumpet sounded, the star *had* fallen. "Had" in this sense depicts a past,

---

81   For evidence that stars represent God's people or angels, see Daniel 12:3 and Job 38:6, 7. For evidence that stars can also represent fallen angels, see Isaiah 14:12 and Revelation 12:4 and 7–9.

completed action, so the star was already on the earth at the time John saw it. This fits Satan exactly because he was cast out of heaven shortly before the creation of the world and again at or shortly after the crucifixion/resurrection/ascension of Christ (see Rev. 12:10–12; Luke 10:18).

- The star in Revelation 9:1 is given the key to the Abyss. A parallel passage in 20:1–3 makes it clear that the Abyss will be the abode of Satan and his angels during the millennium (see Luke 8:30, 31).
- The king of the locusts in the fifth trumpet is called Abaddon in Hebrew and Apollyon in Greek (see verse 11)—Hebrew and Greek words that mean "destroyer."[82] Satan is the destroyer. While Revelation doesn't say so, it seems like a reasonable, educated guess to conclude the fallen star in verse 1 and the king in verse 11 are one and the same.

Putting all the evidence together, I believe there is every reason to identify the star in Revelation 9:1 that had fallen from the sky to the earth as Satan.

The Abyss

The next question we need to address is the nature of the Abyss. There are several references to the Abyss in Revelation. In Revelation 9 verses 1 and 2, the star, Satan, is given the key to the Abyss, and he uses the key to open the Abyss and release a large swarm of locusts. However, at some future time, the key is taken away from him and given to an angel who, after Christ's second coming, uses the key to open the Abyss, bind Satan, and cast him into it. Then he locks and seals it so Satan can't deceive people ("the nations") anymore (see Rev. 20:1–3).

From what we've read thus far, it appears that the Abyss is a place, and this seems to be confirmed by an incident in the life of Jesus. He and His disciples crossed the Sea of Galilee in a boat one day, and they landed at "the region of the Gerasenes" (Luke 8:26). However, they had no more than gotten out of the boat when a ferocious-looking man who was stark naked ran toward them. Jesus commanded the evil spirit to come out of him—it turned out to be a whole legion of evil angels (see verse 30), and they "begged Him repeatedly not to order them to go into the Abyss" (verse 31). Therefore, again, the Abyss seems to be a place. Two other

---

82 Don F. Neufeld, ed., Seventh-Day Adventist Bible Dictionary (Washington, DC: Review and Herald, 1960), vol 8, pp. 2, 59.

texts in Revelation confirm the idea of the Abyss being a place from which demonic figures emerge. Revelation 11:7 and 17:8 both speak of a beast power, which is clearly demonic, that comes up from the Abyss.

With this in mind, what is the "Abyss," and perhaps more importantly, *where* is it? Every text we've read thus far suggests it's a place where demons "dwell." Some people probably think it's in the heart of the earth; others, that it's on the moon or perhaps the planet Jupiter or even in the Bermuda Triangle. However, I'm going to suggest it isn't a place at all; rather, it's a *condition*—the condition of being invisible to humans. How many people reading this book have ever seen a demon? Raise your hand if your answer is "Yes." I suspect very few, if any, readers of this book raised their hands. That's because God has placed a restraint on the demonic forces in the world to prevent them from appearing to humans as demons or supernatural beings, except under very limited conditions, as when humans give themselves up to the demons. The demoniac Jesus encountered on the other side of the Sea of Galilee is a good example of someone who had allowed demons to take control of his life.

However, inspiration makes it very clear that a day is coming when this restraint over the human race will be removed and demonic forces will be allowed to appear openly to humans. Paul spoke about this in 2 Thessalonians 2. He described an antichrist figure—what he called "the man of lawlessness"—who will be revealed at the very end of time and said the second coming of Christ cannot take place until this man of lawlessness is revealed (see verses 1–3). He also said the man of lawlessness "will oppose and will exalt himself over everything that is called God or is worshipped, so that he sets himself up in God's temple, proclaiming himself to be God" (verse 4). The ultimate fulfillment of this prediction will take place when Satan appears visibly to human beings as Christ.[83]

Paul went on to say, "Don't you remember that when I was with you I used to tell you these things? And now you know what is holding him back, *so that he may be revealed at the proper time*" (verses 5, 6, emphasis added). At the present time, something or someone is restraining Satan and his demonic forces from appearing openly to human beings. I believe the one putting that restraint on Satan is God—perhaps the Holy Spirit. However, Paul said this restraint will be removed:

> *And then the lawless one will be revealed,* whom the Lord Jesus will overthrow with the breath of his mouth and destroy by the splendor

---
83 See White, *The Great Controversy*, p. 624.

of his coming. The coming of the lawless one will be in accordance with how Satan works. He will use all sorts of displays of power through signs and wonders that serve the lie, and all the ways that wickedness deceives those who are perishing. (2 Thess. 2:8–10, emphasis added)

Please notice the following pattern in everything I've said about the Abyss and the lawless one:

- In Luke 8:31, we learned the Abyss is a "place" to which demons who possessed the demoniac didn't want to be forced to return.
- Revelation 11:7 and 17:8 tell us that at the very end of time, a demonic "beast" power will "come up" out of the Abyss.
- Revelation 9:1, 2 tells us that at the sounding of the fifth trumpet, Satan will be given the key to the Abyss, and locusts (demonic beings—more on that in a moment) will come up from the Abyss and torture the wicked.
- Paul spoke about a "lawless one," a satanic power, who will be revealed to the human race at the very end of time and perform great and miraculous signs and wonders to deceive the wicked.

To sum up, at the present time, the world's demonic forces are allowed to *influence* human beings. They can tempt and harass us, but they can't do this openly. They can't appear to humans visibly as supernatural beings. However, a time is coming when these demonic forces will be released to appear openly to human beings all over the planet. That's the meaning of the key to the Abyss that's handed to Satan, the star that falls from the sky in Revelation 9:1, 2. And if what I have said about the first four trumpets is correct, then we can know approximately when these demonic forces will be released to appear openly to humans. It will be *after* the terrible devastation of the first four trumpets.

The Locusts

I suggested a moment ago that the locusts the star releases when he opens the Abyss will be demons. John said when the star opened the Abyss, "smoke rose from it like the smoke from gigantic furnace ... And out of the smoke locusts came down upon the earth and were given power like that of scorpions of the earth" (Rev. 9:2, 3).

Please notice an interesting passage in Luke 10. Jesus had sent out seventy-two of His disciples two by two on a missionary tour, and they returned with a thrilling report. "Lord," they said, "even the demons submit to us in your name" (Luke 10:17).

In reply, Jesus gave the disciples two reasons why the demons were subject to them. First, He said, "I saw Satan fall like lightning from heaven" (Luke 10:18). In other words, Satan is a fallen foe. Notice the similarity between this statement and what John described in the fifth trumpet: "I saw a star that had fallen from the sky to the earth" (Rev. 9:1). When Jesus said He saw Satan fall from heaven like lightning, He was explaining why the disciples could cast out demons. Satan and his demons had no power over the disciples. And this is Jesus' second point: the disciples *did* have power over the demons. He said, "I have given you authority to trample on snakes and scorpions and to overcome all the power of the enemy; nothing will harm you" (Luke 10:19).

The serpent has been a demonic symbol since the beginning of time (see Gen. 3:15). In the Luke passage, Jesus also makes scorpions a demonic symbol. This is additional evidence that the locusts in the fifth trumpet, whose home is the Abyss, are demons. Notice the following similarities between an army of locusts described in Joel 2 and the locusts described in Revelation 9:

The locusts in Joel 2	The locusts in Revelation 9
1. "The day of the LORD is a day of … darkness and gloom, a day of clouds and blackness" (verses 1, 2).	1. "The sun and sky were darkened by the smoke from the Abyss" (verse 2).
2. [The locusts] have the appearance of horses; they gallop along like cavalry" (verse 4).	2. "The locusts looked like horses prepared for battle" (verse 7).
3. "[The nation that invades Israel] has the teeth of a lion" (1:6).	3. "Their teeth were like lions' teeth" (verse 9).
4. "With a noise like that of chariots they leap over the mountaintops … Like a mighty army drawn up for battle" (2:5).	4. "The sound of their wings was like the thundering of many horses and chariots rushing into battle" (verse 9).

Next, please notice the activity of these locusts (i.e., demons):

> They were told not to harm the grass of the earth or any plant or tree, but only those people who did not have the seal of God on their foreheads. They were not given power to kill them, but only to torture them for five months. And the agony they suffered was like that of the sting of a scorpion when it strikes a man. During those days men will seek death, but will not find it; they will long to die, but death will elude them. (Rev. 9:4–6)

Satan will not be allowed to afflict God's people during the fifth trumpet, but the torment he and his evil hosts inflict upon the wicked will be so terrible that they will long to die. There's a biblical parallel for suffering imposed by Satan that's so intense that the sufferer longs for death. Notice what Job said when Satan was allowed to afflict him with terrible sores: "Why is light given to those in misery, and life to the bitter of soul, to those who long for death that does not come, who search for it more than for hidden treasure?" (Job 3:20, 21).

Apparently the demons who appear to human beings won't be pleasant. Are we to suppose, however, the demons will torment the very ones who are on their side—those who don't have the seal of God?[84] That's hardly the way to win friends and influence people! But remember that Satan is a cruel liar and deceiver, and so does not have the capacity to be kind, even to his own followers.

Please notice the following quote from the pen of inspiration, which I believe explains Revelation's prediction:

> While appearing to the children of men as a great physician who can heal all their maladies, [Satan] will bring disease and disaster, until populous cities are reduced to ruin and desolation. Even now he is at work. In accidents and calamities by sea and by land, in great conflagrations, in fierce tornadoes and terrific hailstorms, in tempests, floods, cyclones, tidal waves, and earthquakes, in every place and in a thousand forms, Satan is exercising his power. He sweeps away the ripening harvest, and famine and distress follow. He imparts to the air a deadly taint, and thousands perish by pestilence. These visitations are to become more and more frequent and disastrous. Destruction will be upon both man and beast ...

---

84 For a brief study about "the seal of God," see Appendix C.

And then the great deceiver will persuade men that those who serve God are causing these evils.[85]

The only explanation I can give you for why Satan torments his own people during the fifth plague is that he, as Ellen White suggests, will do so secretly, then persuade the world that God's people are responsible for the suffering the wicked are experiencing. Can you imagine the intense anger this will arouse against God's people? Perhaps this is one of the factors that will prompt the wicked, after the close of probation, to issue a death decree for the saints.

Continuing with the fifth trumpet, John's description of this symbolic army of locusts, representing demons, is very weird:

> The locusts looked like horses prepared for battle … their faces resembled human faces. Their hair was like women's hair, and their teeth were like lions' teeth. They had breastplates like breastplates of iron, and the sound of their wings was like the thundering of many horses and chariots rushing into battle. (Rev. 9:7–9)

I don't think we should try to figure out what each of these details means because I'm not sure they have that much meaning. I suspect John is simply trying to give us a very terrible impression. If there is a specific meaning to these details, we'll have to wait to find out what it is.

How Will Satan Appear?

Satan never appears to human beings as Satan. He always disguises himself. What disguise will he use when he appears, as predicted by the fifth trumpet? The Bible doesn't say, but I think a bit of educated guessing about the times in which we live can give us a good clue.

If the first four trumpets indeed destroy the world's ecology, as I have suggested, then the world will be desperate for answers. Think of the horror of a family watching their house burn down. After these four trumpets have "sounded," the whole world will stand in horror at the terrible devastation that has come on the earth. Human beings, recognizing their survival as a race is threatened (see Matt. 24:21, 22), will be grasping for solutions—some way—*any* way—out of the desperate situation in which they struggle.

---

85 White, *The Great Controversy*, pp. 589, 590 (emphasis added).

Furthermore, I expect earth's inhabitants will recognize the calamities that are devastating their plant as "acts of God" and turn to their religious leaders for a spiritual solution. Ecumenism will happen on a global scale. Even the Arabs and Israelis will make their peace! However, what solution can the religious leaders offer?

Enter Satan—ET (extraterrestrial). He and his angels will claim to be intelligent beings from another part of our galaxy or perhaps a distant galaxy in the universe. They will present themselves as an advanced race of beings who have overcome similar problems and offer their "help." Their help will be spiritual as well as physical, and of course, the whole world will be searching for spiritual answers.

While this scenario is speculative, it fits well with the culture in which we live today. Hollywood bombards us with fictional movies about outer space and extraterrestrials, and the scientific community has been searching the heavens with radio telescopes for decades, hoping to find some hint of intelligent communication from another part of the universe. Satan would have to be naïve in the extreme not to take advantage of this opportunity to deceive the human race. It's my personal conviction that he is the one putting the play writers and scientists up to all this in the first place for the very purpose of using it when the time is right.

The reason why scientists have not yet made contact with these "extraterrestrials" is very simple: so far, God hasn't allowed Satan and his angels to escape from the Abyss. They still are not allowed to make direct contact with human beings. However, if my interpretation of the fifth trumpet is correct, then in the not-too-distant future, Satan will be released following the series of terrible natural disasters in the first four trumpets that devastate our planet. At that time, the scientific instruments located all over the world will come alive with "evidence" that contact has been made with extraterrestrials.

The Time Period

Perhaps you wonder what the prophecy means when it says the demons will be allowed to torture the wicked for five months. *The New International Version Study Bible* has a footnote to this time period: "*Five months.* A limited period of time suggested by the life cycle of the locust or the dry season (spring through late summer, about five months), in which the danger of a locust invasion is always present."[86]

---

86 *The NIV Study Bible*, note on Rev. 9:5.

Whether we are to understand this time period to be more than an allusion to the life cycle of the locust in the spring and summer, I cannot say at this time. The fact that it's mentioned twice (Rev 9:5, 10) suggests it's more than a mere allusion—it *does* have significance. Five months of symbolic time, according to the year/day principle, would be 150 years of literal time. I hardly think the world will last another 150 years at the time the trumpets are sounding, so if by the five months we are to understand an actual time period, I believe it should be understood as literal time. However, I will have more to say about this in a later chapter.

To sum up, the fifth trumpet is the appearance of demonic forces in the aftermath of the global devastation that's caused by the first four trumpets. It is true, then, that this will be the time during the final crisis when the spiritualism Ellen White so often predicted in her writings will take place.

Chapter 11

The Sixth Trumpet

The sixth trumpet is closely related to the fifth. It's also more terrible than any of the previous trumpets:

> The sixth angel sounded his trumpet, and I heard a voice coming from the four horns of the golden altar that is before God. It said to the sixth angel who had the trumpet, "Release the four angels who are bound at the great river Euphrates." And the four angels who had been kept ready for this very hour and day and month and year were released to kill a third of mankind. The number of the mounted troops was twice ten thousand times ten thousand. I heard their number. The horses and riders I saw in my vision looked like this: Their breastplates were fiery red, dark blue, and yellow as sulfur. The heads of the horses resembled the heads of lions, and out of their mouths came fire, smoke and sulfur. A third of mankind was killed by the three plagues of fire, smoke and sulfur that came out of their mouths. The power of the horses was in their mouths and in their tails; for their tails were like snakes, having heads with which they inflict injury. The rest of mankind who were not killed by these plagues still did not repent of the work of their hands; they did not stop worshiping demons, and idols of gold, silver, bronze, stone and wood—idols that cannot see or hear or walk. Nor did they repent of their murders, their magic arts, their sexual immorality or their thefts. (Rev. 9:13–21)

The golden altar, from which came the voice that John heard, was without a doubt the same golden altar he saw in his vision in Rev. 8:3–5, and the angel of the altar would have been the same one who cast the censer to the earth—the action that authorized the seven angels to blow their trumpets. Perhaps the terrible nature of this trumpet helps us to understand why it begins with a voice from the altar: God wants us to understand He is still in command. Terrible as it is, the sixth trumpet does not take Him by surprise. It can only happen with His permission and at His direction. Regardless of how difficult our circumstances may be, God is always in charge of our lives if we allow Him to be. I suspect God's people who are living on the earth at the time of the sixth trumpet will need all the assurance they can get, for they will be sorely tempted to think He has abandoned them. Satan will surely use the opportunity to press that thought upon their minds and emotions.

> *Regardless of how difficult our circumstances may be, God is always in charge of our lives if we allow Him to be.*

If the voice from the golden altar is indeed the angel who ministers at that altar, then we can reasonably say six angels will be involved in the sixth trumpet:

The angel at the golden altar	One angel
The angel who blows the sixth trumpet	One angel
The angels who are bound at the River Euphrates	Four angels

The Four Angels

Who are these four angels, and what is the River Euphrates where they are bound? Our sense of biblical parallels suggests these four angels may be the same four angels who hold back the four winds in Revelation 7:1–3. However, a careful comparison of the two passages makes it clear that this is not the case. When the four angels of chapter 7 are given permission to do their work, they harm the earth's ecology—the land, sea, and trees—whereas the four angels of the sixth trumpet kill a third of the human race. The four angels of chapter 7 stand at the four corners of the earth, whereas the four angels of the sixth trumpet are bound at the River Euphrates.

My personal conclusion is that the sixth trumpet is simply a further description of the demonic forces that were released from the Abyss in the fifth trumpet. At the time the demons were released from the Abyss, they were still somewhat restrained. God told Satan he could torment Job by destroying his property and afflicting his body, but he put on him a restraint: he could not kill Job. The demons from the fifth trumpet can only torment earth's wicked inhabitants. They are held back from killing them. However, in the sixth trumpet, all restraint is removed, and they are permitted to kill a third of the human race.

The Great War

The demons (locusts) in the fifth trumpet are described somewhat in military terms (see Rev. 9:7–9), but in the sixth trumpet, they become a regular army. John said, "The number of mounted troops was two hundred million" (verse 16, CSB). He also said, "I heard their number." This number should probably be understood as symbolic of a vast host rather than as a literal census. In verses 17–19, John described these troops in highly figurative language that's just about as strange as is his description of the troops in the fifth trumpet. I have no more burden to try to decipher every symbolic detail of the sixth trumpet than I did with the fifth. However, I do believe we can understand the broad sweep of the sixth trumpet.

I've suggested the first four trumpets are ecological disasters that will strike the earth. I've also suggested the fifth trumpet is the release of Satan and his demons to appear visibly to the human race, and at that time, they will be allowed to torment the wicked but specifically forbidden to do any more ecological damage (see verse 4). If these conclusions are correct, then in the sixth trumpet, Satan and his angels will be allowed to organize an army and bring great trouble on the earth.

Chapter 12

The Mighty Angel of Revelation 10

Before we get into a discussion of Revelation 10, let's take a moment to review the first six trumpets. Revelation 8 describes the first four trumpets, which bring a series of devastating calamities upon the world. Trumpet number five is about a great star (a symbol of Satan) that had fallen from the sky to the earth. The star is given permission to open up the Abyss, which is the abode of demons, and release demonic forces, symbolized by a swarm of locusts, to harm the wicked. God's people, those who had "the seal of God on their foreheads" (Rev. 9:4), are specifically protected from that harm. Finally, trumpet number six is about a great war these demonic forces will unleash upon the world. Now, here's a point I want you to notice: With the exception of the protection from these demonic forces that God's people receive, the first six trumpets say *nothing* about God's people. However, as you will see in a moment, that changes with Revelation 10 and the first half of chapter 11.

> **With the exception of the protection God's people receive, the first six trumpets say nothing about God's people.**

It's also important to note, as I pointed out in a previous chapter, that Revelation 10 and the first half of chapter 11 constitute an interlude between the sixth and seventh trumpets.

This interlude covers the entire period of the first six trumpets. In this chapter, I will deal with the part of the interlude in Revelation 10, and in the following two chapters, I will deal with the rest of the interlude in Revelation 11:1–13.

Revelation 10 can be divided into three parts. Part 1, verses 1–4, is about a mighty Angel who comes down from heaven holding a little scroll in His hand. In part 2, verses 5–7, the Angel announces the end is near, which means the proclamation of the gospel to the world is almost ended. And part 3, verses 8–11, tells of the bittersweet experience through which God's people will go as they fulfill the Angel's command to give the final proclamation of the gospel to all the world.

The Mighty Angel Who Comes Down from Heaven

Then I saw another mighty angel coming down from heaven. He was robed in a cloud, with a rainbow above his head; his face was like the sun, and his legs were like fiery pillars. He was holding a little scroll, which lay open in his hand. He planted his right foot on the sea and his left foot on the land, and he gave a loud shout like the roar of a lion. When he shouted, the voices of the seven thunders spoke. And when the seven thunders spoke, I was about to write; but I heard a voice from heaven say, "Seal up what the seven thunders have said and do not write it down." (Rev. 10:1–4)

A key question we need to settle is the identity of this mighty Angel. I'm sure you've noticed by now that I've capitalized the word "Angel," together with any pronoun that refers to Him (He, Him, and His). This is a clear indication that I consider Him to be a divine Being—namely, Jesus Christ. My reason for this conclusion is the glorious description of Him in verses 1 and 2: He has a rainbow above His head, His face shines like the sun, His legs are like fiery pillars, and the sound of His voice is like the roar of a lion. This description is similar to the one in Revelation 1:12–16 of "a son of man" (verse 13), who, of course, is Jesus. And Ellen White confirmed the conclusion that this Angel is Jesus: "the mighty angel who instructed John was no less a personage than Jesus Christ."[87]

Revelation 10:2 says the Angel is "holding a little scroll, which lay open in his hand." What is this little scroll? Daniel was told to "close up and seal the words of the scroll until the time of the end. Many will go here and there to increase knowledge" (Dan. 12:4). Daniel's scroll contained the total history of every nation and individual who has ever lived, and God's interventions on their behalf. I believe the scroll the Angel in Revelation 10

---

[87] White, *The SDA Bible Commentary*, vol. 7 (Washington, DC: Review and Herald Publishing Association, 1957), p. 971.

is holding in his hand is the scroll Daniel was told to close up.[88] Please note the relevant quotes below:

> There in His open hand lay the book, the roll of the history of God's providences, the prophetic history of nations and the church. Herein was contained the divine utterances, His authority, His commandments, His laws, the whole symbolic counsel of the Eternal, and the history of all ruling powers in the nations. In symbolic language was contained in that roll the influence of every nation, tongue, and people from the beginning of earth's history to its close.
>
> This roll was written within and without. John says: "I wept much, because no man was found worthy to open and to read the book, neither to look thereon" [verse 4]. The vision as presented to John made its impression upon his mind. The destiny of every nation was contained in that book. John was distressed at the utter inability of any human being or angelic intelligence to read the words, or even to look thereon. His soul was wrought up to such a point of agony and suspense that one of the strong angels had compassion on him, and laying his hand on him assuringly, said, "Weep not: behold, the Lion of the tribe of Juda[h], the Root of David, hath prevailed to open the book, and to loose the seven seals thereof" [verse 5].
>
> John continues: [verses 6, 7, quoted]. As the book was unrolled, all who looked upon it were filled with awe. There were no blanks in the book. There was space for no more writing. [Revelation 5:8-14; 6:8-11; Revelation 8:1-4, quoted.][89]
>
> "Shall I crucify your King?" Pilate asked, and from the priests and rulers came the answer, "We have no king but Caesar" (John 19:15). [...]
>
> Thus the Jewish leaders made their choice. Their decision was registered in the book which John saw in the hand of Him that sat upon the throne, the book which no man could open. In all its

---

88 Dr. George Knight, a former chairman of the Church History Department at the Seventh-day Adventist Theological Seminary in Berrien Springs, Michigan, wrote a 26-page paper titled, "The Controverted Book of Revelation 10 and the Shape of Apocalyptic Mission," in which he provided conclusive evidence that the scroll in the Angel's hand is the scroll Daniel was told to seal "until the time of the end" (Dan. 12:4).

89 White, *Manuscript Releases*, vol. 12, pp. 296, 297.

vindictiveness this decision will appear before them in the day when this book is unsealed by the Lion of the tribe of Judah.[90]

We've already noted that the whole context of the seven trumpets is end-time events, which means it's time for Daniel's scroll about the end time to be progressively better understood. In fact, it began to open with many conservative Protestant interpreters beginning in the late 1700s and early 1800s, culminating with William Miller and the early Seventh-day Adventists. And it's continued right up to the present, especially with Seventh-day Adventists.

Let's take a moment to reflect on the significance of this Angel, who is Jesus, coming down to the earth and planting His feet on the sea and land. Jesus left this earth nearly 2,000 years ago when He ascended to heaven, and the two angels who appeared to His disciples told them specifically He would come back in the clouds of heaven "in the same way you have seen him go into heaven" (Acts 1:11). However, His appearance in Revelation 10, in which He comes down and plants His feet firmly on this earth and sea, cannot be His second coming. It's a symbolic "appearance" for the purpose of bringing a special message to God's people as they confront the devastating calamities of the first four trumpets and the demonic forces of the fifth and sixth trumpets.

The Final Proclamation of the Gospel

The rest of chapter 10 is about the final proclamation of the gospel:

> Then the angel I had seen standing on the sea and on the land raised his right hand to heaven. And he swore by him who lives forever and ever, who created the heavens and all that is in them, the earth and all that is in it, and the sea and all that is in it, and said, "There will be no more delay! But in the days when the seventh angel is about to sound his trumpet, the mystery of God will be accomplished, just as he announced to his servants the prophets." (Rev. 10:5–7)

In this section of Revelation 10, the Angel makes an extremely important announcement—so important that He does it in the same way judges in today's world require of people who testify in court: He raises His right hand to heaven and swears by God, except His oath is much more elaborate than are any in today's courts. He swears "by him who lives for ever

---

90 White, *Christ's Object Lessons*, pp. 293, 294. (Cf. Rev. 20:11-15; book unsealed.)

and ever, who created the heavens and all that is in them, and the earth and all that is in it, and the sea and all that is in it." Therefore, whatever it is the Angel is about to say, it's *extremely important!* His announcement consists of six words—*just six words!* What can He say in just six words that deserves this elaborate oath? *"There Will Be No More Delay!"*

The meaning of "there will be no more delay." The King James Version quotes the Angel saying, "There shall be *time* no longer" (emphasis added). From the beginning of our movement, Seventh-day Adventists have interpreted this to mean there will be no more time prophecies. The 1,260 years and 2,300 years are the last time prophecies that have ever been given or will be given. Uriah Smith interpreted the angel's statement that "there shall be time no longer" to mean that "no prophetic period should extend beyond the time of this message"—that is, "beyond the autumn of 1844."[91] Additionally, "Seventh-day Adventists ... have understood the 'time' to be prophetic time, and its end to signify the close of the longest time prophecy, that of the 2300 days of Dan. 8:14. After this there is to be no further message bearing on a definite time. No time prophecy extends beyond 1844."[92]

However, as we've already noted, the New International Version that I'm using here has the angel saying, "there will be no more delay," and all the other major versions of the Bible over the past seventy-five years agree, including the NKJV, NRSV, and NASB.

In my view, "no more delay" fits the context of Revelation 10 better than does "time no longer." I say this for a couple reasons: First, the traditional Adventist interpretation that there will be no more definite time prophecies after 1844 doesn't fit the context. The whole point of Revelation 10 is an announcement that the final proclamation of the gospel has begun, and God isn't going to extend it much longer. This is especially evident in verse 7, which we will examine in a moment.

Second, interpreting the KJV translation, "There should be time no longer," to mean there will be no more time prophecies beyond 1844 is an imposition of that view *onto* the text. Nothing in the context or wording of the sentence itself suggests this idea. On the other hand, the wording "there will be no more delay" fits the context perfectly," as we shall now see.

Verse 7 says, "in the days when the seventh angel is about to sound his trumpet, the mystery of God will be accomplished, just as he announced to his servants the prophets." What is this "mystery of God"?

---

91   Smith, p. 525.
92   Nichol, *The Seventh-day Adventist Bible Commentary*, vol. 7, p. 798.

Paul made the answer to this question very clear. "Pray also for me, that whenever I speak, words may be given me so that I will fearlessly make known *the mystery of the gospel,* for which I am an ambassador in chains. Pray that I may declare it fearlessly, as I should" (Eph. 6:19, 20, emphasis added). Paul said the mystery of God is the gospel. However, the gospel as words in the Bible is meaningless unless it's proclaimed, which is precisely what Paul said—twice. First, he asked the Ephesian Christians to pray "that whenever I open my mouth, words may be given me so that I will fearlessly make known" this "mystery of the gospel," and then he said, "Pray that I may declare it fearlessly, as I should" (see also Eph. 3:2–6; Rom. 16:25, 26).

Finally, Revelation 10:7 says the mystery of God will be finished "in the days when the seventh angel is about to sound his trumpet." By this, He means the proclamation of the gospel will continue only a short time longer. This fits perfectly with the previous verse, where the Angel proclaimed, "there will be no more delay." The proclamation of the gospel has been going on since the Garden of Eden in Genesis 3:15, and especially since Jesus began proclaiming it during His earthly ministry. His apostles proclaimed it throughout the New Testament period, and God's people throughout the centuries have proclaimed it. However, that proclamation is almost over. It will be "accomplished"—that is, completed—finished—when the seventh angel sounds his trumpet.

We come now to the third and final section of Revelation 10 that we will be discussing in this chapter:

> Then the voice that I had heard from heaven spoke to me once more: "Go, take the scroll that lies open in the hand of the angel who is standing on the sea and on the land." So I went to the angel and asked him to give me the little scroll. He said to me, "Take it and eat it. It will turn your stomach sour, but in your mouth it will be as sweet as honey." I took the little scroll from the angel's hand and ate it. It tasted as sweet as honey in my mouth, but when I had eaten it, my stomach turned sour. Then I was told, "You must prophesy again about many peoples, nations, languages and kings." (Rev. 10:8–11)

Verse 8 is simply a command from a voice in heaven (see verse 4) for John to take the little scroll from the hand of the Angel. In verse 9, John followed through by asking the Angel to give him the scroll. The Angel handed him the scroll with the instruction that he should eat it, but with the warning that "it will turn your stomach sour, but in your mouth it will be as sweet as honey."

The pioneers of the Seventh-day Adventist Church took these words very personally, and that's quite understandable. The message of the soon coming of Jesus was indeed very sweet to them during the Advent movement of early 1844, but they were devastated when He failed to arrive on October 22. Describing that experience, Hiram Edson said, "Our fondest hopes and expectations were blasted, and such a spirit of weeping came over us as I never experienced before. It seemed that the loss of all earthly friends could have been no comparison. We wept and wept, till the day dawn."[93] However, I believe the book that's sweet in the mouth but sour in the stomach will be fulfilled to a much greater extent during the world's final crisis.

Verse 11 says, "Then I was told, 'You must prophesy again about many peoples, nations, languages and kings.'" Notice John was told that he was to prophesy "*about* many peoples, nations, languages and kings" (emphasis added). That seems rather odd to me. Why would the Angel tell him to preach *about* all these people? I prefer the King James Version's translation: "Thou must prophesy again *before* many peoples, and nations, and tongues, and kings" (emphasis added). "Either meaning suits the context."[94] The Angel's command to John is actually a repetition of the great commission Jesus gave to His disciples shortly before He left the earth, which was to "go and make disciples of all nations" (Matt. 28:19). Therefore, in Revelation 10:11, the Angel, Jesus, is repeating His commission in an end-time setting for His end-time people. It's essentially the same commission as that of the that first angel in Revelation 14:7, who "had the eternal gospel to proclaim to those who live on the earth—to every nation, tribe, language and people."

Overview of Revelation 10

Let's conclude this discussion of Revelation 10 by bringing all the pieces together. Jesus comes to earth as a mighty Angel, plants His right foot on the sea and His left foot on the land, which suggests that whatever reason He had for coming to the earth, its purpose is global. It's for the entire human race, not just for one nation.

---

93 Arthur L. White, *Ellen White: The Early Years* (Hagerstown, MD: Review and Herald Publishing Association, 1985), p. 53.
94 Nichol, *The Seventh-day Adventist Bible Commentary*, vol. 7, p. 799.

The first thing the Angel says when He speaks is "there will be no more delay!" (verse 6). However, He doesn't just *say* it. He raises His hand to heaven and swears an oath "by him who lives for ever and ever, who created the heavens and all that is in them, the earth and all that is in it, and the sea and all that is in it" (verse 6). That is some oath! It means that we, the readers, should take it very, *very* seriously.

What is this delay that won't continue much longer? Verse 7 gives us the answer: "In the days when the seventh angel is about to sound his trumpet, the mystery of God will be accomplished, just as he announced to his servants the prophets." We learned earlier in this chapter that the mystery of God is the gospel, the message about eternal salvation in His heavenly kingdom for those who believe in Jesus and commit their lives to Him.

However, John is warned that while the message itself is as sweet as honey, proclaiming it will be a bitter experience. Why? Because of the fierce opposition which those who proclaim the message will face, though Revelation 10 doesn't tell us about that fierce opposition. For that, we have to wait for chapter 11, which I will be covering in the next two chapters, especially focusing on the two witnesses who will proclaim this end-time message. All John told us about the message is that he must proclaim it "before many peoples, and nations, and tongues, and kings."

Chapter 13

My Understanding of the Two Witnesses

In Revelation 10, which we discussed a couple chapters back, we learned about a mighty Angel, Jesus Christ, who symbolically comes down to earth, plants His feet firmly on the sea and land, and declares, "there will be no more delay" (verse 6). By this, Jesus means the time has come for the final proclamation of the gospel message (see verse 8), which will take place a short time before He assumes dominion over the kingdoms of the world and reigns "forever and ever" (Rev. 11:15). And to conclude chapter 10, the Angel repeats the great commission He gave to His disciples 2,000 years ago, albeit worded differently. "Thou must prophesy again before many peoples, and nations, and tongues, and kings" (verse 11, KJV). I find it significant that this same gospel commission is repeated in the first angel's message (see Rev. 14:6, 7), underscoring the fact that this commission is an urgent part of the work of God's end-time people.

Now I'll share with you my understanding of the two witnesses in Revelation 11:1–6. I'll begin by reminding you that 10:11 and 11:1, 2 are very closely linked. Some commentators have even suggested the division between chapters 10 and 11 should have started with 11:3.

Revelation 11:1, 2 are about the end-time judgment, and, as I mentioned in the previous chapter, this theme is an important part of the Adventist end-time message (see Rev. 14:6, 7). That is probably the reason why many Seventh-day Adventist prophetic interpreters consider it to be closely associated with 10:11. However, interpreting 11:1, 2 as the judgment is as far as the traditional Adventist interpretation of 11:1–13 takes the *end-time* proclamation of the gospel. As I pointed out in the previous chapter, because of the 42 months/1,260 days, we've reverted to the proclamation of the gospel by the two witnesses during the Middle Ages, A.D. 538–1798.

Now I'd like to invite you to partake in a bit of imaginary interpretation with me. Suppose the 42 months/1,260 days were not included as a part of Revelation 11:2, 3. We can't remove them, of course, but for the sake of making my point, how would Adventists interpret the testimony of the two witnesses in verses 4–13 if the two time periods were not there? My answer is we would view the testimony of the two witnesses as the *final* proclamation of the gospel during the time of the end, not as its proclamation during the Middle Ages.

The themes of "no more delay," "the mystery of God [being] accomplished," and prophesying "before many peoples, nations, languages, and kings" (Rev. 10:6, 7, 11) would flow seamlessly from chapter 10 through the first half of chapter 11 without any interruption in the time element. And frankly, I believe this is what the Angel who inspired these two chapters intended, and it will be fulfilled during the world's final crisis just before the close of probation.

I agree with the view that the two witnesses represent the Old and New Testaments (i.e., the Bible). I add to this the observation that the two witnesses have to be *more* than the Old and New Testaments. The Bible as a book is of no more value than a dictionary or any other book if all it does is lie on a shelf. The Bible has to be picked up and read, and if it's going to be of any value in carrying out Christ's great commission, it has to be used by God's people as the basis of their witness to the world. Therefore, the two witnesses in Revelation 11 are more than just the Old and New Testaments as a book. I agree with the following statement:

> The two witnesses represent the people of God. In the New Testament, witnessing is the primary task of God's people. Jesus often referred to His disciples as witnesses (cf. John 15:27; Luke 24:48). Before His ascension, Jesus made this clear to His disciples: "You shall receive power when the Holy Spirit has come upon you; and you shall be My witnesses both in Jerusalem and in all Judea and Samaria, and even to the remotest part of the earth" (Acts 1:8; cf. 2:32; 3:15; 5:32). According to Jesus, the preaching of the gospel before the end is "for a witness to all the nations" (Matt. 24:14). In Revelation, witnessing is the reason why God's people are persecuted (2:13; 6:9; 12:11; 17:6; 20:4). It is the church that bears witness to Jesus.[95]

Even the Old Testament commissioned the Hebrew nation to witness (Isa. 43:10-12 and 44:8).

---

95   Stefanovic, pp. 352, 353.

My conclusion, then, is the two witnesses of Revelation 11:3–13 are symbolic of the people of God who proclaim the everlasting gospel to the world during the time of the seven trumpets, which is the final crisis.

The Two Witnesses and the First Six Trumpets

At this point, I'm going to take a break from the testimony of the two witnesses to consider the context in which they will proclaim their message. Keep in mind that the entire prophecy about the seven trumpets in Revelation 7–11 is a unit that includes the interlude in chapter 10 and the first half of chapter 11. This means the two witnesses will proclaim their end-time gospel (1) during the time of the calamities and natural disasters of the first four trumpets, (2) in the face of the demonic forces of the fifth and sixth trumpets, and (3) during the persecution by the forces of evil arrayed against them. I'll begin with their proclamation of the gospel during the period of the first four trumpets.

1. Proclaiming the gospel during a time of calamities and natural disasters. The Bible's predictions of calamitous events is hardly limited to the first four trumpets. Paul said, "While people are saying, 'Peace and safety,' destruction will come on them suddenly" (1 Thess. 5:3). In the context of the falling of the stars, Luke told us, "the nations will be in anguish and perplexity" and "men will faint from terror, apprehensive of what is coming on the earth" (Luke 21:25, 26). And Jesus warned us that "great distress" will come upon earth's final generation that is "unequaled from the beginning of the world till now." In fact, it will get so bad that "if those days had not been cut short, no one would survive" (Matt. 24:21, 22).[96]

Can you imagine calamities so severe that they would threaten the survival of the human race? No wonder Luke said the nations will be in anguish and perplexity and the human race will faint from terror!

Ellen White wrote more about the destructive forces of nature during the end time between 1895 and 1905 than in any other period in her life. For example, "O that God's people had a sense of the impending destruction of thousands of cities, almost given to idolatry"; "The time is near when large cities will be swept away."[97] Then there's her vision in which she saw "great balls of fire [that] were falling upon houses … The terror of the

---

[96] While none of these texts say anything about the proclamation of the gospel in these difficult circumstances, we are justified in inserting it because the gospel will continue to be proclaimed until the close of probation, shortly before Christ returns.
[97] White, *Evangelism*, 29.

people was indescribable."[98] That reminds me of the first trumpet: "hail and fire mixed with blood ... hurled down upon the earth" (Rev. 8:7).

Finally, there's Ellen White's interpretation of Luke 21:25: As a result of the signs in the sun, moon and stars, "Nations will be in anguish and perplexity at the roaring and tossing of the sea," which she interpreted to be "the sea and the waves ... pass[ing] their borders"[99]—in other words, tsunamis. This suggests large meteorites and possibly asteroids will smash into our planet. And, as we learned in Revelation 8, that's precisely the gist of the first three trumpets.

White made it clear that God's people will be proclaiming the final warning to the world during this tumultuous time.

> The Lord will not suddenly cast off all transgressors or destroy entire nations; but He will punish cities and places where men have given themselves up to the possession of Satanic agencies. Strictly will the cities of the nations be dealt with, and yet they will not be visited in the extreme of God's indignation, because *some souls will yet break away from the delusions of the enemy, and will repent and be converted,* while the mass will be treasuring up wrath against the day of wrath.[100]

There are Biblical clues that the trumpets may be part of the close of probation. Other Biblical clues seem to indicate that the trumpets may precede its close. Some overlapping may occur. White didn't say anything about the proclamation of the gospel by God's people in this statement, but that's how these people will come to "break away from the delusions of the enemy"; it's how they will "repent and be converted." It will be the testimony of the two witnesses during the period of the first four trumpets that will bring them to accept Jesus as their Savior.

2. Proclaiming the gospel during a time of demonic forces warring against God's people. To complicate matters a thousandfold, the two witnesses will have to proclaim their testimony during a period of intense demonic opposition. The fifth trumpet describes demonic forces that will be unleashed on the world during this time. Revelation 9:1 tells of "a star that had fallen from the sky to the earth," which nearly all commentators interpret to represent Satan, and I agree. God will give Satan the key to the Abyss, which is the abode of demons (see Luke 8:30, 32; Rev. 20:1–3).

---

98 *Ibid.*
99 White, *Selected Messages*, book 3, p. 417.
100 White, *Evangelism*, p. 27 (emphasis added).

The significance of this is that throughout the history of sin on our planet, God has held that key and placed a restraint on how much open contact demons were allowed to have with humans. However, at the very end of time, God will give Satan the key to the Abyss, and he will use it to open this dwelling place of demons and release upon the world hordes of these devilish beings, who are represented in Revelation as locusts. In this final short segment of the great controversy between good and evil, these demonic forces will interact with human beings in ways they have never been able to do heretofore[101].

> **At the end, God will give Satan the key to the Abyss, and he will use it to release upon the world hordes of demons.**

Ellen White confirmed this. One of the major emphases in all of her writings about the final crisis is the prominent role spiritualism (communication with demons) will have during this time. For instance, she gave a perfect example of demons confronting average human beings in ways they have not been permitted to do at any time previously in earth's history:[102]

> Many [people] will be confronted by the spirits of devils [im]personating beloved relatives or friends and declaring the most dangerous heresies. These visitants will appeal to our tenderest sympathies and will work miracles to sustain their pretensions. We must be prepared to withstand them with the Bible truth that the dead know not anything and that they who thus appear are the spirits of devils.[103]

Revelation predicts all of this close interaction between demonic beings and humans in the fifth trumpet.

The sixth trumpet describes a huge war that will involve the entire world. Revelation 13 also speaks of this war. The beast that rises from the sea will "make war *against the saints* and ... conquer them" (verse 7, emphasis added). And the beast that rises from the land will set up an image to the beast that rises from the sea, and God's people who will refuse

---

101 See White, *The Great Controversy*, p. 588.
102 This is exemplified in Revelation by the release of the locusts from the abyss under the fifth trumpet. As I pointed out earlier in this chapter, prior to the time of the final crisis, the demons have been restricted in their ability to appear personally to the average person.
103 White, *The Great Controversy*, p. 560.

to worship the beast will be threatened with death (see verses 14, 15).[104] The land beast will also put a mark on the entire human population, except for God's people, who refuse to accept the mark; they will be denied the right to buy or sell (see verses 16, 17).

3. Proclaiming the gospel during a time of opposition from the wicked. A third part of the context in which the two witnesses will proclaim their message is persecution by those who oppose them. This is described in Revelation 11:2 and 5. Verse 2 says the Gentiles (i.e., the wicked) will trample on the holy city for forty-two months. The holy city is symbolic of the dwelling place of God's people all over the world, and trampling on them means persecuting them. Additionally, "if anyone tries to harm [the two witnesses], fire comes from their mouths and devours their enemies" (verse 5). The point in both of these verses is that the two witnesses have enemies who will oppose them and try to stop their proclamation of the gospel message. Ellen White had a great deal to say about this. In the following quotes, she spoke of the efforts by the world to oppose God's people who are proclaiming the final warning:

> Wealth, genius, education, will combine to cover [God's people] with contempt. Persecuting rulers, ministers, and church members will conspire against them. With voice and pen, by boasts, threats, and ridicule, they will seek to overthrow their faith.

> There will come a time when, because of our advocacy of Bible truth, we shall be treated as traitors.

> Those who honor the Bible Sabbath will be denounced as enemies of law and order, as breaking down the moral restraints of society, causing anarchy and corruption, and calling down the judgments of God upon the earth. Their conscientious scruples will be pronounced as obstinacy, stubbornness, and contempt of authority. They will be accused of disaffection toward the government.[105]

I invite you to compare these sentiments expressed against God's people during the final crisis with what is going on in the world right now. The contempt vented by liberals against conservatives and vice versa is a small taste of the contempt that will be thrust on God's people during the final crisis. Trampling by the Gentiles and prophesying in sackcloth are mild manifestations compared to the reality they will face.

---

104 There will be martyrs during the time of the final warning, but not all of God's people will be killed.
105 White, *Last Day Events*, pp. 146, 147.

The Power of the Two Witnesses

With all that said, how on earth can the two witnesses ever proclaim their end-time gospel message under this kind of harsh opposition? Revelation 11:3 answers that question: "I will give power to my two witnesses, and they will prophesy for 1,260 days clothed in sackcloth." The sackcloth, as I pointed out in the previous chapter, represents the painful difficulty the two witnesses will have to endure as they bear their testimony to the world, but two factors will make it possible for them to do this.

The first factor is the Holy Spirit, who is represented by the two olive trees and two lampstands. I pointed out in a previous chapter that these two symbols come from Zechariah 4:1–6, and when the prophet asked his angel what the olive trees and lampstands represented, the angel replied, "This is the word of the LORD, to Zerubbabel: 'Not by might nor by power, but by my Spirit,' says the LORD Almighty" (verse 6).

Later in chapter 4, the angel told Zechariah the lampstand represents "the two who are anointed to serve the LORD of all the earth" (verse 14). This fits perfectly with the two witnesses in Revelation 11. They are the olive trees and lampstands, not because they *are* the Holy Spirit, but because the Holy Spirit possesses them, which makes them His ministers—His agents to proclaim the final gospel message to the world.

The second factor that will make it possible for the two witnesses to proclaim their message with power in spite of intense persecution will be the Angel in Revelation 10, who came down from heaven and planted His feet firmly on the sea and earth. He will also be with His people during this difficult time. It's because of the presence of Jesus Christ and the Holy Spirit in the lives of the two witnesses that "if anyone tries to harm them, fire comes from their mouths and devours their enemies. This is how anyone who tries to harm them must die" (Rev. 11:5). These words, of course, are symbolic of the power God's people will have during the final crisis—not the power to physically destroy those who oppose them but the spiritual power to counter the efforts of their enemies to stop them from proclaiming the final warning.

"These men have power to shut up the sky so that it will not rain during the time they are prophesying; and they have power to turn the waters into blood and to strike the earth with every kind of plague as often as they want" (verse 6). Two powers or abilities are mentioned here. The first one, the power to shut up the sky so it will not rain, reminds us of Elijah, who told King Ahab, "there will not be dew nor rain in the next few years except at my word" (1 Kings 17:1), and the second one reminds us of Moses, through whom God turned water into blood and brought ten devastating plagues on the land of Egypt (see Exod. 7–11). Elijah's curse came down upon the apostate people of God, and Moses' curse came down upon the pagan Egyptians.

Similarly, during the final conflict, God's Spirit will give His people ways to counteract the attacks of their enemies that we probably don't understand today, and the forces of evil will not be able to destroy their witness. Ellen White illustrated this truth:

> Many reformers, in entering upon their work, determined to exercise great prudence in attacking the sins of the church and the nation. They hoped, by the example of a pure Christian life, to lead people back to the doctrines of the Bible. But the Spirit of God came upon them as it came upon Elijah, moving him to rebuke the sins of a wicked king and an apostate people; they could not refrain from preaching the plain utterances of the Bible—doctrines which they had been reluctant to present … The words which the Lord gave them they uttered, fearless of consequences, and the people were compelled to hear the warning.
>
> Thus the message of the third angel will be proclaimed. As the time comes for it to be given with greatest power, the Lord will work through humble instruments, leading the minds of those who consecrate themselves to His service. The laborers will be qualified rather by the unction of His Spirit than by the training of literary institutions.
>
> Men of faith and prayer will be constrained [by the Spirit] to go forth with holy zeal, declaring the words which God gives them.[106]

This energizing power of the Holy Spirit to proclaim God's end-time message to the world is symbolized in Revelation 11:3, 4 by the two olive trees and two lampstands, which Zechariah said represent the mighty power of the Holy Spirit (4:1–6).

The Testimony of the Two Witnesses Ends

"Now when [the two witnesses] have finished their testimony, the beast that comes up from the Abyss will attack them, and overpower and kill

---
106 White, *The Great Controversy*, p. 606.

them" (Rev. 11:7). The first clause means the mission of the two witnesses is over. They now cease their proclamation of the gospel. This is a clear indication that probation has closed because as long as probation is open, there is the possibility that some people might accept the message of the two witnesses and be saved.

Verse 7 goes on to say a beast that arises from the Abyss will attack the two witnesses and kill them. The beast that arises from the Abyss will be a demonic power, though it is not specifically identified as Satan himself.[107] The killing of the two witnesses refers to their message, not to them personally, because Ellen White has assured us there will be no martyrs after the close of probation. "If the blood of Christ's faithful witnesses were shed at this time, it would not, like the blood of the martyrs, be as seed sown to yield a harvest for God … It would be a triumph for the prince of darkness."[108]

If I'm correct that the finishing or completion of the testimony of the two witnesses represents the close of probation, then the rest of the interlude (see Rev. 11:8–13) represents the time of trouble. However, I don't claim to understand everything about these verses. We will have to wait until the events foretold here begin to develop in order to understand them more fully.

Now it's time to look at the 42 months/1,260 days in the context of being fulfilled during the world's final crisis.

---

107 Revelation 17:8 also speaks of a beast that "will come up out of the Abyss." We can assume the same demonic power is in mind in both references.
108 White, *The Great Controversy*, p. 634.

Chapter 14

The Two Time Periods of Revelation 11

I pointed out in the previous chapter that the biblical evidence persuades me to believe the 42 months/1,260 days of Revelation 11:2, 3 and the 42 months of 13:5 have to be understood as a literal three-and-a-half years. In this chapter, I will share with you my reasons for this conclusion.

The Angel told John the Gentiles would "trample on the holy city for 42 months" (Rev. 11:2). This same time period occurs in 13:5, where the beast that rises from the sea is allowed to "exercise his authority for 42 months." The 42 months in both Revelation 11 and 13 have to do with a period of time that's given to the wicked. On the other hand, in 11:3, God's two witnesses, the righteous, will "prophecy for 1,260 days, clothed in sackcloth." These two time periods, while stated differently, are actually identical, because 42 months of 30 days each[109] equal 1,260 days. Thus, I suggest the wicked trampling on the holy city for 42 months means they will persecute God's people during that time, and during this same time, His people, the two witnesses, will be dressed in sackcloth, which, as I pointed out in a previous chapter, is a biblical symbol of sadness and mourning. Thus, at the same time the wicked are persecuting the righteous for proclaiming God's end-time message, the righteous are enduring suffering, sadness, and mourning.

Seventh-day Adventists have always identified the 1,260 days of Daniel 7:25 and Revelation 12:6 and 14[110] as symbolic of 1,260 years rather than literal days, and I agree with that interpretation in these two chapters. However, interpreting the seven trumpets as future end-time events, as I am presenting them in this book, creates a problem. How can we work 1,260 *years* into the end time? We obviously can't. However, if the trumpets truly are future events, as I've argued in this book, then the 1,260 days/42

---

109 In ancient Jewish reckoning, each month had thirty days, and every few years, a leap month was added to keep the calendar year in synchronization with the solar year.

110 Revelation 12:14 uses the words "time, times, and half a time," which are the same words in Daniel 7:25 that also mean 1,260 days.

months in Revelation 11 and 13 have to be understood as 1,260 *literal* days and 42 *literal* months—that is, three-and-a-half *literal* years. I believe a strong case can be made for this interpretation.

The Time Periods in Revelation 11:2, 3

The first thing we have to keep in mind is Revelation 10 and the first half of 11 (the interlude between the sixth and seventh trumpets) are a unit. Therefore, in order to understand the two time periods of Revelation 11, we need to consider them in the context of the interlude as a whole. Therefore, let's begin with Revelation 10.

The context. Revelation 10 begins with a mighty Angel who descends from heaven holding a small scroll in His hand, and the scroll is opened. This reminds us of what Daniel was told: "seal the words of the scroll until the time of the end" (Dan. 12:4). I agree with those who suggest the open scroll in the Angel's hand is the sealed scroll of Daniel that is now unsealed. This is a clear indication that the Angel of Revelation 10 has a message for God's end-time people.

> **The theme of Revelation 10 is the proclamation of the gospel during the end time, which will be both sweet and bitter.**

Then the Angel declares there will be "no more delay" (Rev. 10:6). He means the mission of the church, which began with Christ's great commission almost 2,000 years ago, is about to be completed. This is confirmed by what the Angel said next: "But in the days when the seventh angel is about to sound his trumpet, the mystery of God will be *accomplished*, just as he announced to his servants the prophets" (verse 7, emphasis added). The mystery of God is the plan of salvation—what the Bible calls "the gospel" (see Eph. 6:19; Rom. 16:25, 26). Therefore, the *accomplishment* of the mystery of God is the final proclamation of the gospel.

Following this, John was told to eat the scroll the Angel held in His hand, and when he did this, "it tasted as sweet as honey in my mouth, but when I had eaten it, my stomach turned sour" (Rev. 10:10). Then John was told he must "prophecy again before many peoples, and nations, and tongues, and kings" (KJV). This is Christ's great commission in an end-time setting. Therefore, the theme of Revelation 10 is the proclamation of the gospel during the end time, which will be both a very sweet and very bitter experience—sweet because the gospel is such good news for sinners yet bitter because of the persecution against those who proclaim it.

With this context in mind, let's now move forward in Revelation.

Revelation 11:1–6. The first two verses about measuring the temple and the worshipers refer to the judgment-hour message, and then come the 42 months, during which the Gentiles will trample on the holy city, and the 1,260 days, during which God's two witnesses will be given power to prophecy while clothed in sackcloth (verses 2–6). The trampling of the holy city by the Gentiles is a symbol of the persecution of God's people who proclaim this judgment-hour message, which is why the two witnesses prophesy in sackcloth. This reminds us again of the bitter taste John experienced when he ate the little book the Angel handed him.

Now I'd like you to engage in a bit of imaginary interpretation with me. Let's just suppose the 42 months/1,260 days were not included as a part of Revelation 11:2, 3. Of course, we can't remove those two time periods from the Bible, but for the sake of our present argument, let's leave them out temporarily. Given the context I've just outlined in Revelation 10, how would you interpret the prophesying of the two witnesses in chapter 11? I propose that without the two time periods, there would be no need to revert to the medieval era for our interpretation of the two witnesses. Instead, the two witnesses would represent the proclamation of the gospel "before many peoples, nations, tongues, and kings" (Rev. 10:13, KJV) in an end-time setting. Their prophesying while "clothed in sackcloth" would represent the proclamation of the gospel during the persecution of the final crisis. However, the end time is such a short period that there's no way to work 1,260 years into it—at least we sincerely hope not!

All of Revelation 10 is about the proclamation of the gospel without delay at the very end of time, and it's in the context of the proclamation of the two witnesses in 11:1–6. This is the reason why I understand the two time periods for the proclamation by the two witnesses to be a literal three-and-a-half years, not a symbolic 1,260 years.

The Time Period in Revelation 13:5

While Revelation 13 is outside the purview of the seven trumpets, I'm including it here because it also mentions 42 months, and I find the evidence for a literal end-time interpretation of those months in Revelation 13 to be even stronger than it is in Revelation 11. I will share with you three reasons for this conclusion: (1) again, the context; (2) the healing of the fatal wound; and (3) the relationship between the sea beast and the land beast.

The context. I find the same logic applicable to the 42 months in Revelation 13 that I shared with you regarding the 42 months/1,260 days of Revelation 11:2, 3. Revelation 12 provides the *context* for the interpretation of Revelation 13, just as Revelation 10 provides the context for Revelation 11. Therefore, let's look at Revelation 12.

Verses 1–5 are about a woman who gives birth to a child, and a great red dragon tries to kill the Child as soon as He is born. The dragon is Satan (see verse 9), and the Child is Jesus. Thus, the chapter begins with Christ's birth and Herod's effort to have Him killed. However, the Child is "snatched up to God and his throne," which happened at Christ's ascension (see verse 5). Having lost the opportunity to destroy Jesus while He was on earth, Satan pursues the woman, who symbolizes the Christian church.

However, God protects the woman by preparing a place in the desert where she can be "taken care of for 1,260 days" (verse 6), and she "was given the two wings of a great eagle, so that she might fly to the place prepared for her in the wilderness, where she could be taken care of for a time, times and half a time" (verse 14). Seventh-day Adventists have always understood both of these time periods in Revelation 12 to apply to the 1,260 years from A.D. 538 to 1798, and I'm in full agreement with that interpretation because they clearly have to do with the history of the Christian church, beginning with the time of the apostles.

"From his mouth the serpent [another name for the dragon—see verse 9] spewed water like a river, to overtake the woman and sweep her away with the torrent" (verse 15). This symbolizes the fact that Satan's intention was to persecute the medieval Christian church so severely, it would be blotted from the earth. However, "the earth helped the woman by opening its mouth and swallowing the river that the dragon had spewed out of his mouth" (verse 16). Seventh-day Adventists have traditionally interpreted this to symbolize the opening up of the new world in the late 1500s and early 1600s, which provided a way of escape for Protestants who were being persecuted in Europe, and I find this to be a satisfactory explanation of these two verses. Therefore, Revelation 12:1–16 is a snapshot of Christian history from the time of Christ to the opening up of "the new world" on the North American continent.

Then we come to verse 17: "the dragon [Satan] was enraged at the woman and went off to make war against the rest of her offspring, those who obey God's commandments and hold to the testimony of Jesus." Seventh-day Adventists have always understood this verse to refer to God's end-time church, which (1) keeps all of God's commandments, including the fourth, and (2) has the "testimony of Jesus"—that is, the "spirit of prophecy" (Rev. 19:10), which refers to the gospel proclamation, including the prophetic ministry of Ellen White.

This is the context we need for understanding the 42 months in Revelation 13:5. Now let's apply the same logic here that we did in chapters 10 and 11. How would we interpret Revelation's description of the sea beast's activities if there were no 42 months in verse 5? I suggest we would understand the sea beast's activities to be a further description of the dragon's fierce attack on the woman in Revelation 12:17. However, the 42 months have forced us to ignore this context and revert back to the period from A.D. 538 to 1798. However, we just covered that time period with the 1,260 days and the time, times, and half a time in Revelation 12, so why repeat it in chapter 13?

It seems to me that the two beasts in Revelation 13 are an additional description of the dragon's *end-time* attack on the woman about which we read in 12:17. Chapter 13 simply picks up this end-time persecution of the woman in 12:17 and expands on it. That's why I say the context of the beast from the sea in Revelation 12, especially verse 17, suggests the 42 months in chapter 13:5 should be understood as literal time, not symbolic time.

The fatal wound. My second reason for interpreting the 42 months in verse 5 as literal time is the fatal wound in verse 3, which says one of the heads of the beast from the sea "seemed to have had a fatal wound." We have always interpreted this wound to represent the French army's arrest of Pope Pius VI in February 1798. However, this needs a bit more background in order to understand the full meaning of the fatal wound and its healing.

What was the significance of Pope Pius's arrest and his exile to France? It meant that at that point, the papacy had totally lost the political and religious authority over the European nations it had held for many centuries. It's important to understand, however, that the papacy's loss of political power wasn't a single event in February 1798. That loss took several centuries to develop.

The papacy achieved the height of its political power between about 1200 and 1500.

However, two trends began in the late 1400s and early 1500s that started the papacy's drift toward political insignificance. One was Nicolaus

Copernicus's study of astronomy,[111] which led him to conclude the earth is not the center of the universe. This, of course, contradicted the Catholic Church's firm belief that the earth *was* the center of the universe,[112] but it initiated a trend that led to Western culture being dominated by scientific, rather than religious, authority.

The other trend that weakened papal authority was the Protestant Reformation. The printing press, which Gutenberg invented in the mid-1400s, also contributed greatly to the progress of these two trends because, like today's internet, it made the exchange of ideas much more efficient than it had ever been before.

The papacy fought both the Scientific Revolution and the Protestant Reformation bitterly, especially the latter. However, as time went on, the nations of Europe grew increasingly weary of papal authority, and over a period of several hundred years, they gradually gained the political upper hand. The final blow was the French Revolution, which was a violent rebellion against all religious authority, and it's in this context that Pius VI was arrested and imprisoned. That's why Seventh-day Adventists consider his imprisonment to be "the fatal wound," and I am in full agreement with that interpretation.

However, Revelation 13:3 says, "the fatal wound had been healed" (NIV, NRSV). Please pay careful attention to what I say next: At the time the beast rose from the sea, the deadly wound *had already been healed*. And it's only *after* the wound is healed that the beast is given 42 months to exercise its authority (see verse 5).[113] With that said, what does the healing of deadly wound mean? When does it take place?

In 1929, the papacy signed what's known as the Lateran Treaty with the Italian government, giving the papacy complete political control over about 108 acres in Rome. This territory is known as "Vatican City." Overnight, the

---

111 Nicolaus Copernicus (1473–1543) was a mathematician and astronomer who formulated a model that placed the sun, rather than the earth, at the center of the universe. We now know neither the sun nor the earth is at the center of the universe, but Copernicus's theory was a significant advance over the Ptolemaic theory of the universe that had dominated European thought for a millennium and a half (see https://1ref.us/7t11).

112 The Catholic Church didn't invent the theory that the earth is the center of the universe. It was the brainchild of Claudius Ptolemy (about A.D. 100–168), who was a Greek mathematician, astronomer, and geographer. His idea that the earth was the center of the universe was based on his observation of the stars and planets moving around the earth as the earth turned on its axis. This concept is known as the Ptolemaic theory of the universe (see https://1ref.us/7t12). The Catholic Church adopted this theory, claiming that texts such as Joshua 10:12–13, Psalm 93:1, and Psalm 19:4–6 provided biblical support.

113 Some versions, such as the King James and New King James, say the deadly wound "*was* healed," but either way, it's clear that at the time the beast rose from the sea, the wound had already been healed.

papacy became a "nation" with full, independent authority over those 108 acres. It's the smallest nation in the world, but it *is* a nation. For example, like all other nations, the Vatican exchanges ambassadors with other nations all over the world.

Back in 1929, some Adventists proclaimed that with the Lateran Treaty, the deadly wound had been healed. It's understandable they would conclude this, but it is not correct. Just as the decline in the papacy's political power over Europe took several centuries, so it's taking several decades to grow back into its political power, and that healing is still in progress. The healing of the fatal wound won't be fully completed until the papacy regains its political dominance, not only over Europe, but over the entire world. And Revelation makes it very clear *when* that will happen. The beast power "was given a mouth to utter proud words and blasphemies *and to exercise his authority* for forty-two months" (Rev. 13:5, emphasis added); additionally, the beast power *"was given authority over every tribe, people, language and nation"* (verse 7, emphasis added). In other words, shortly before the end of time, the beast power, the papacy, will become the world's global political and religious authority. Only then will the deadly wound be fully healed, and at the time the beast rose from the sea, the wound had *already* been healed (see verse 3). Therefore, as of the writing of this chapter (April 2020), the deadly wound is still in the healing process because the papacy still has not gained political authority over "every tribe, people, language and nation" (verse 7). However, when it does, it will exercise that authority for 42 months—that is, three-and-a-half literal years.

The fatal wound and its healing, both of which take place *before* the 42 months are mentioned, is an important reason why I believe the 42 months are a literal three-and-a-half years still in the future. Equally significant for drawing this conclusion is the beast that rises from the earth, as we shall now see.

The beast that rises from the earth. Seventh-day Adventists have always understood the beast that rises from the earth to represent the United States, and I agree with that interpretation, though I reach this conclusion for reasons that are different from the traditional approach (see Appendix B). Keep in mind that the United States did not become an independent nation until the late 1700s. Over the next 200 years, it grew in its power until by the year 2000, it was the world's only superpower.[114]

---

114 The United States became a global superpower at the end of World War II, and with the fall of the Soviet Union in the early 1990s it became the world's only superpower. Today both Russia and China are superpowers that are vying to become the world's dominant superpower, but they have not yet

Now please notice a key point: There is a very close relationship between the beast that rises from the earth and the beast that rises from the sea. The beast that rose from the earth "exercised all the authority of the first beast on his behalf and made the earth and its inhabitants worship the first beast, whose fatal wound had been healed" (Rev. 13:12). "It is apparent that the earth beast [i.e., land beast] represents the religiopolitical power *in the service of the sea beast*."[115]

This relationship between the United States and the papacy during the final crisis is similar to the relationship that existed between the papacy and the governments of Europe during the Middle Ages. The papacy had no military power then, and it has no military power today.

During the Middle Ages, the papacy depended on the military power of the nations of Europe to enforce its dogmas on the people, and during the final crisis, it will depend on the military power of the United States to enforce its dogmas on the world. That's why the beast that rises from the earth, the United States, "exercised all the authority of the first beast *on its behalf*" and "*made the earth and its inhabitants worship the first beast*" (Rev. 13:12, emphasis added). We read a moment ago that the first beast "was given authority over ever tribe, people, language and nation," which it will exercise for 42 months. Then we discover that this authority will actually be exercised by the second beast, the United States, "on behalf of" the first beast, the papacy.

Now here is the key point: For the United States to exercise the papacy's authority, the two have to exist simultaneously, and that could only happen *after* 1798, not before.

Verse 13 goes on to say, "[the land beast (i.e., the United States)] performed great and miraculous signs, even causing fire to come down from heaven to earth in the full view of man."[116] Then "because of the signs that he was given power to do *on behalf of the first beast*, he deceived the inhabitants of the world" (verse 14, emphasis added). The point, again, is there is a very close relationship between these two beasts. They interact with each other. This means they have to exist at the same time in earth's history.

However, this would be impossible if the two beasts existed at totally different times. The traditional Adventist interpretation has the first beast

---

reached that status, and if our understanding of the land beast in Revelation 13 is correct, they won't achieve that status.

115 Stefanovic, p. 429 (emphasis added).
116 Some Adventists have said this is a reference to atomic bombs, which the United States invented and introduced into the world. This probably isn't what the text means. It's one of those aspects of apocalyptic prophecy that we won't understand until it's fulfilled.

exercising dominance from A.D. 538 to 1798, which means its political power was diminishing at just the time when the United States was getting its start in the late 1700s. It obviously would be impossible for the United States to have been the enforcement arm of the papacy during the Middle Ages. The papal beast *has* to exist alongside the United States beast in order for the United States to assist the papacy in exercising its authority.

This is why I believe the 42 months of the papal beast's authority has to be literal.

Conclusion

Let's summarize what I've shared with you in this chapter. First, the contexts of Revelation 10–13 provides strong evidence that the time periods in those chapters should be understood literally as three-and-a-half years. In Revelation 10 and 11, the Angel declares the delay is almost over and the mystery of God is about to be accomplished—that is, Jesus' great commission is about to be finished. Then the Angel basically repeats that commission to John. The two witnesses proclaim this end-time great commission clothed in sackcloth (see Rev. 11:16), which reminds us of the sour stomach John experienced when he ate the little book the Angel handed him. It just seems to me that Revelation 10 and 11 are a unit that predicts the final and painfully difficult proclamation of the gospel during the end time.

The same thing happens in Revelation 12 and 13. Chapter 12 is a summary of the dragon's persecution of the Christian church during the 1,260 days and the time, times, and half a time—that is, the 1,260 years from A.D. 538 to 1798. Then the angry dragon concentrates all his wrath in a furious attack on God's end-time church, and this is followed immediately by the appearance of a beast from the sea that is given great authority to persecute God's people. In other words, this beast from the sea is a further elaboration of the dragon's furious attack on the woman in Revelation 12:17.

The respective contexts of Revelation 10 and 11, and of 12 and 13, both suggest the time periods in these chapters should be understood literally as a part of the end-time persecution of God's people.

Then Revelation 13 provides two other strong pieces of evidence that the 42 months of verse 5 should be understood as literal time. First is the timing of the fatal wound that was inflicted on the beast that rose out of the sea: It was healed in verse 3 *before* the beast was given 42 months to exercise his authority and *before* verse 7, when the beast is given authority to rule the world. Second is the close relationship that exists between the sea beast and land beast. In order for the land beast to exercise all the authority of the sea beast, the two have to exist simultaneously. It would be impossible for the land beast (the United States) to assist the sea beast (the papacy) between A.D. 538 and 1798 because the United States didn't exist during that period.

There's one more issue we need to discuss with respect to everything I've said so far in this book: Does Ellen White have anything to contribute to the discussion? That will be the topic of the next chapter.

Chapter 15

What Ellen White Said About the First Six Trumpets

Ellen White was one of the world's preeminent Christian influencers during the second half of the nineteenth century and the early twentieth century. The world does not recognize this, but I consider it a privilege to have been born and raised in a Seventh-day Adventist home that led me to accept her inspired writings. In spite of the fact that she had only a third-grade education and an injury while in the third grade that nearly cost her her life, Ellen White's seventy-year, heaven-guided ministry resulted in the formation of the Seventh-day Adventist Church. Today it has the largest missionary presence around the globe compared to other Protestant denominations. Our church also has the largest global educational system, publishing ministry, and medical ministry of all Protestant denominations.

In 1850, just five years after the Great Disappointment, the United States had a population of a little over 23 million people.[117] A conservative estimate of William Miller's followers prior to October 22, 1844, would be around 100,000. That's about 0.4 percent of the nation's population, which may not sound like a lot. However, a single religious leader in today's America, which has an estimated 341 million people,[118] would have to garner nearly 1.5 million adherents in order to equal William Miller's percentage of the American population in 1850. Yet so profound was the disappointment following October 22, 1844, that only about 100 of Miller's followers maintained their confidence in Christ's second coming and the calculation of 1844 as the conclusion of the 2,300-day/year prophecy. And Ellen White was one of the prominent leaders of this small group, which resulted in today's Seventh-day Adventist Church, with some 22 million members.

---

117 See "1850 United States census," Wikipedia Foundation, last modified November 15, 2021, 17:14. https://1ref.us/7t13.
118 https://1ref.us/7t14.

There is no doubt in my mind that God gave Ellen White the prophetic gift. I consider her writings to have been inspired by the Holy Spirit in the same way the authors of the Bible were inspired in the production of their writings. The difference between their writings and hers is not in the quality or degree of inspiration. The difference is one of authority. She herself emphasized repeatedly that the Bible and the Bible only is to be the authoritative basis for our teachings.

However, her writings provide great insight into what the Bible says, especially with regard to the cosmic conflict; the war between good and evil that began in heaven and has raged on our planet for approximately 6,000 years. And, as you know from reading what I've said so far in this book, I believe the seven trumpets have to do with the final part of that conflict shortly before the second coming of Jesus. So let's find out what Ellen White had to say about the first six trumpets. I'll begin with the first four.

The First Four Trumpets

I'm aware of only one statement Ellen White made that could be understood as a significant reference to the first four trumpets:

> Solemn events before us are yet to transpire. *Trumpet after trumpet is to be sounded;* vial after vial poured out one after another upon the inhabitants of the earth. Scenes of stupendous interest are right upon us.[119]

The Fifth and Sixth Trumpets

On the fifth and sixth trumpets, the White Estate website gives four references to her comments. However, in two of them, she said nothing about these two trumpets as far as I could tell, and the other two, in which she commented on the sixth trumpet, are identical.

I will share Ellen White's comment with you later in this chapter, but for now, we need to read the part of the sixth trumpet on which she commented, and I will follow this with some historical background,

---

[119] White, *Selected Messages*, book 3, p. 426 (emphasis added). I read all of page 405, and she referred to the three angels' messages and the message of the mighty angel in Revelation 18:1–3, but for the life of me, I couldn't find anything resembling a reference to the first four trumpets.

which you will need in order to understand her comment on the passage:

> The sixth angel sounded, and I heard a voice from the four horns of the golden altar which is before God, saying to the sixth angel which had the trumpet, Loose the four angels which are bound in the great river Euphrates. And the four angels were loosed, which were prepared for an hour, and a day, and a month, and a year, for to slay the third part of men. (Rev. 9:13–15, KJV)[120]

These verses made a deep impression on William Miller's followers prior to October 22, 1844. I will give you some historical background that will help you understand their thinking.

The Roman Empire. The emperor Constantine ruled the Roman Empire from A.D. 306 to his death in 337. During his reign, he moved the capital of the empire from Rome to a city in what is now Eastern Turkey called Byzantium, which he renamed Constantinople. The Roman Empire was now divided into two parts: the western part, with its capital in Rome, and the eastern part, with its capital in Constantinople. The Western Roman Empire came to an end in A.D. 476, when several barbarian tribes invaded the city of Rome and conquered it. However, the eastern empire continued for several more centuries.

One of the challenges the eastern empire faced was the rise of the Islamic religion in the Middle East in the early 600s. By the year 700, Muslims ruled the Middle East and much of North Africa. In a crucial battle on July 27, 1299, the Muslims' Ottoman Empire defeated the Eastern Roman Empire and established their capital in Constantinople, which they renamed Byzantium. Numerous commentators on Revelation, including William Miller and his associates, considered the fifth and sixth trumpets in Revelation chapter 9 to represent the Ottoman Empire.

The Ottoman Empire. You will recall that in the fifth trumpet, the locusts that had been released from the Abyss "were told not to harm the grass of the earth or any plant or tree, but those only who did not have the seal of God[121] on their foreheads. They were not given power to kill them, but only to torture them *for five months*" (Rev. 9:4, 5, emphasis added). Based on the year-for-a-day principle, the Millerites concluded this represented 150 years of time.

---

120 Ellen White didn't interpret these verses herself. She adopted the interpretation of Josiah Litch, as did her associates following the Great Disappointment, especially Uriah Smith.
121 For a brief study about "the seal of God," see Appendix C.

The sixth trumpet also includes a time prophecy. A voice from the golden altar in heaven commands the angel holding the sixth trumpet to "loose the four angels in the great river Euphrates. And the four angels were loosed, who were prepared *for an hour, and a day, and a month, and a year,* to slay the third part of men" (verses 14, 15, emphasis added). Our pioneers calculated that the hour, day, month, and year represented 391 years and 15 days. They then combined the 150 years in the fifth trumpet with the 391 years and 15 days in the sixth trumpet for a total 541 years and 15 days, which they interpreted as the period of the Ottoman Empire's rule. They understood 150 years to represent the *rise* of the Ottoman Empire and the 391 years and 15 days to represent its *domination*.

The Millerites. Josiah Litch, who was one of the predominant Millerite preachers, used July 27, 1299, as the beginning date for the rise of the Ottoman Empire because that is when the crucial battle occurred between the Ottoman Turks and the Eastern Roman Empire, which resulted in an Ottoman victory.

> **Litch's announcement attracted widespread attention as the world's attention was focused on negotiations between the Ottoman Empire and Western powers.**

With the specific date of July 27, 1299, for the beginning of the Ottoman Empire, it was simple enough to calculate the end of the 541 years and 15 days: September 11, 1840. Litch initially predicted the Ottoman Empire would fall sometime *during* the month of August, but a few days before August 11, he announced the empire's power would be broken *on that day*. Given the great public interest in the calculation by an early Adventist of Christ's return sometime in 1843 or early 1844, Litch's announcement attracted widespread attention, especially given the fact that at that time, the world's attention was focused on negotiations that were going on between the Ottoman Empire and Britain, France, Austria, Prussia, and Russia. These Western powers were challenging the Ottoman Empire's authority, and as August 11 approached, the Millerites waited with bated breath to see what would happen on that day.

Of course, news from the other side of the globe wasn't broadcast the day it happened like it is today, but probably sometime in mid-to-late August, word reached the United States that something occurred on

August 11 that the Millerites considered to be the "fall" of the Ottoman Empire. Here's an explanation:

> On that day [August 11, 1840] the Turkish emissary, Rifat Bey, arrived at Alexandria [Egypt] with the terms of the London Convention. On that day also the ambassadors of the four powers received a communication from the sultan [of the Ottoman Empire] inquiring as to what measures were to be taken in reference to the circumstances vitally affecting his empire. He was told that "provision had been made," but he could not know what it was. Litch interpreted these events as a recognition by the Turkish government [the Ottoman Empire] that its independent power was gone ...
>
> These events, coming at the specified time of Litch's prediction, exercised a wide influence upon the thinking of those in America who were interested in the Millerite movement. Indeed, this prediction by Litch went far to give credence to other, as yet unfulfilled, time prophecies—particularly that of the 2300 days—which were being preached by the Millerites.[122]

Adventist commentators since 1844. Following the Great Disappointment and the establishment of the Seventh-day Adventist Church, our students of prophecy have commented significantly on the 150 years in Revelation 9:5 and the 391 years and 15 days in verse 15. Uriah Smith strongly supported Litch's conclusion.[123] He took seventeen pages to discuss the sixth trumpet, with about half of them devoted to Litch's conclusions about the Ottoman Empire's rise and fall.

Though not commenting on the hour, day, month, and year, one source states, "Generally speaking, the Seventh-day Adventist interpretation of the fifth and sixth trumpets, particularly as touching the time period involved, is essentially that of Josiah Litch."[124]

Mervyn Maxwell supported Litch's conclusion that the hour, day, month, and year, combined with the 150 days in the fifth trumpet, represent the period of the Ottoman Empire's domination of the Middle East and North Africa.[125]

On the other hand, Ranko Stefanovic says that the hour, day, month, and year in Revelation 9:15 "can be understood as 'a divinely appointed

---

122 Nichol, *The Seventh-day Adventist Bible Commentary*, vol. 7, pp. 795, 796.
123 See Smith, pp. 500–517.
124 Nichol, *The Seventh-day Adventist Bible Commentary*, vol. 7, p. 796.
125 Maxwell, pp. 255, 256, 262–265.

moment in time.'"[126] Please note a significant difference of interpretation between Stefanovic and the other commentators. Smith and Maxwell viewed the hour, day, month, and year in Revelation 9:15 as a *period* of time, whereas Stefanovic considers this reference to time to represent a *moment*, or, perhaps more correctly, a *point* in time. Why the difference? And which one is correct? A careful examination of Revelation 9:15 in the original language has convinced most biblical scholars that the words "hour," "day," "month," and "year" should be translated as a *point in* time, not a *period of* time. This is especially evident in the NIV: "And the four angels who had been kept ready *for this very* hour and day and month and year were released to kill a third of mankind" (emphasis added).

With this background, we are ready to examine what Ellen White said about the time part of Revelation 9:15. She gave strong support to Josiah Litch's and Uriah Smith's interpretation of the hour, day, month, and year:

> In the year 1840 another remarkable fulfillment of prophecy excited widespread interest. Two years before, Josiah Litch, one of the leading ministers preaching the second advent, published an exposition of Revelation 9, predicting the fall of the Ottoman Empire. According to his calculations, this power was to be overthrown "in A.D. 1840, sometime in the month of August;" and only a few days previous to its accomplishment [Josiah Litch] wrote: "Allowing the first period, 150 years, to have been fulfilled before Deacozes ascended the throne by permission of the Turks, and that the 391 years, 15 days, commenced at the close of the first period, it will end on the 11th of August, 1840, when the Ottoman power in Constantinople may be expected to be broken. And this, I believe, will be found to be the case" ....
>
> At the very time specified, Turkey, through her ambassadors, accepted the protection of the allied powers of Europe, and thus placed herself under the control of Christian nations. The event exactly fulfilled the prediction .... When it became known, multitudes were convinced of the principles of prophetic interpretation adopted by Miller and his associates, and a wonderful impetus was given to the advent movement. Men of learning and position united with Miller, both in preaching and in publishing his views, and from 1840 to 1844 the work rapidly extended.[127]

---

126 Stefanovic, p. 317.
127 White, *The Great Controversy*, pp. 334, 335.

Here's the problem: Ellen White interpreted the hour, day, month, and year in Revelation 9:15 as a period of time when we now know it actually refers to a point in time. The question is, why did God allow her to support Josiah Litch's interpretation of the hour, day, month, and year as a period of time when these words refer to a point in time? Why did He allow her to give what we recognize to be an incorrect interpretation of this passage?

My Response

A quick search on the White Estate website shows that Ellen White commented a great deal on the seven churches and said quite a bit about the seven seals. However, I find it very significant that she had almost nothing to say about the seven trumpets, and I have to ask myself, 'Why?' My suggestion is the time had not yet come for the future interpretation of these trumpets to be understood by God's people because they apply to a time that was more than a century away from the time in which the early Adventists lived. The trumpets were not "present truth" for that time. Therefore, God did not find it necessary to help Ellen White to understand them. Knowing she and the other pioneers of the Advent movement were extremely interested in the Bible's apocalyptic prophecies, including the seven trumpets, He allowed them to interpret these prophecies as periods of history rather than as a point of time in the future. However, if my interpretation of the trumpets as futuristic is correct, as I believe it is, then the seven trumpets *are* present truth for our time.

Nevertheless, aren't prophets supposed to tell the truth? Can't we trust them to give us correct information about the writings of the prophets that preceded them? Actually, there's nothing new about prophets saying things that turn out to be incorrect. We see the same thing in both the New Testament and the Spirit of Prophecy. I'll begin with several examples from the Bible.

> *I propose that God had a couple of very good reasons for allowing the apostles to think Jesus' return was "just around the corner."*

The New Testament. Consider the following: "The Lord's coming is near ... The Judge is standing at the door" (James 5:8, 9). "The end is near" (1 Peter 4:7). Jesus Himself said three times, "Behold, I am coming soon"; "Behold I am coming soon"; *"Yes, I am coming soon"* (Rev. 22:7, 12, 20, emphasis added). Yet it's been nearly 2,000 years, so how soon is soon? Why did God allow His apostles to be so wrong in promising their readers Jesus would be returning in their day?

I propose that God had a couple of very good reasons for allowing the apostles to think Jesus' return was "just around the corner."

God always adapts His future plans to the readiness or unreadiness of His people. We call this "conditional prophecy." Note the following two quotes:

> Then the word of the Lord came to me. He said, "Can I not do with you, Israel, as this potter does?" declares the Lord. "Like clay in the hand of the potter, so are you in my hand, Israel. If at any time I announce that a nation or kingdom is to be uprooted, torn down and destroyed, and if that nation I warned repents of its evil, then I will relent and not inflict on it the disaster I had planned. And if at another time I announce that a nation or kingdom is to be built up and planted, and if it does evil in my sight and does not obey me, then I will reconsider the good I had intended to do for it. (Jer. 18:5-10)

> Had the purpose of God been carried out by His people in giving to the world the message of mercy, Christ would, ere this, have come to the earth, and the saints would have received their welcome into the city of God.[128]

What do you suppose the Bible writers would have thought had they known His second coming would be put off for 2,000 more years? I can tell you what their response would have been: It would have shaken their faith and crushed their evangelistic fervor!

Ellen White. I believe God raised up the Seventh-day Adventist Church for the very purpose of preparing the world for the second coming of Jesus. Our pioneers who came out of the Great Disappointment also understood that, and they, like the New Testament apostles, believed that Jesus' second coming would happen in the next few years. It was in 1856, just twelve years after the Great Disappointment, when Ellen White made the famous statement to a group of Advent believers that some of those present would be "food for worms"—that is, they would die—while others would be "subjects of the seven last plagues, [and]

---

128 White, *Testimonies for the Church*, vol. 6, p. 450.

some will be alive and remain upon the earth *to be translated at the coming of Jesus.*"[129]

Throughout the rest of her life, Ellen White repeatedly assured her readers and listeners that they had very little time left to prepare for the time of trouble and the second coming of Jesus. She quoted Paul almost word for word: "There has been a decline in the true missionary spirit among ministers and teachers. Yet Christ's coming is nearer than when we believed."[130] This was published in 1889, when the Adventist Church had been in existence for twenty-six years. Why did White, like the apostles, predict to her audiences and readers that Jesus' second coming would take place within their lifetimes?

Again, I propose that had they known that 175 years after the Great Disappointment, God's people in the Western world and much of the Eastern world would still be living relatively complacently, it would have all but crushed their evangelistic zeal.

This, for me, is the best explanation for why God allowed our early Seventh-day Adventist believers to adopt Josiah Litch's interpretation that the seven trumpets symbolized *periods* of time covering nearly 2,000 years. It's why He allowed them to interpret the 150 days in Revelation 9:5 and the hour, day, month, and year in verse 15 to represent a period of 541 years and 15 days that ended on August 11, 1840, rather than a point in time that was still future. I also propose that this is why He gave Ellen White so little information about the seven trumpets. He knew that part of Revelation applied to a time 100–150 years in the future—and who knows how much longer in our own day?

Now let's find out what Ellen White said about the interlude between the sixth and seventh trumpets. First, take just a moment and reread Revelation 10:1 through 11:14.

The Interlude

Ellen White was very traditional in her understanding of the interlude. She said very little about the mighty Angel of Revelation 10, but she commented at length on the two witnesses in chapter 11. I'll begin with what she *did* say about the Angel.

---

129 White, *Testimonies for the Church*, vol. 1 (Mountain View, CA: Pacific Press Publishing Association, 1868), pp. 131, 132 (emphasis added).
130 White, *Testimonies for the Church*, vol. 5, p. 88.

The mighty Angel of chapter 10. White identified this Angel as "no less a personage than Jesus Christ. Setting His right foot on the sea, and His left upon the dry land, shows the part which He is acting in the closing scenes of the great controversy"; it "signifies the wide extent of the proclamation of the message. It will cross the broad waters and be proclaimed in other countries, even to all the world."[131] Interestingly, she suggested that the seven thunders, which the Angel told John not to write down (see Rev. 10:4), were "a delineation of events which [will] transpire under the first and second angels' messages"—that is, "future events *which will be disclosed* in their order."[132] As far as I know, very few Seventh-day Adventist commentators have commented on the meaning of the seven thunders.

Ellen White also commented on the Angel's declaration that "there should be time no longer" (Rev. 10:6), which our pioneers understood to mean there will be no more time prophecies after 1844. She said, "the people will not have another message upon definite time. After this period of time, reaching from 1842 to 1844, there can be no definite tracing of the prophetic time. The longest reckoning reaches to the autumn of 1844."[133] I will have more to say about this in the next chapter.

Ellen White didn't comment on the Angel's commission to John to carry out a global proclamation of the gospel. She simply used His words to encourage her fellow Adventists to proclaim the global message. Here is one example: "The last warning is to be proclaimed 'before many peoples, and nations, and tongues, and kings;' and the promise is given, 'Lo, I am with you always, even unto the end of the world.'"[134]

The two witnesses of chapter 11. Ellen White had much more to say about the two witnesses than she did about the Angel. I will begin with the measuring of the temple in verses 1 and 2. She clearly accepted the view that this had to do with the judgment in heaven. However, in the following quote, she wasn't so much explaining the text as she was applying it to the spiritual life of the Christian:

> The grand judgment is taking place, and has been going on for some time. Now the Lord says, Measure the temple and the worshipers thereof. Remember when you are walking the streets about your business. God is measuring you: when you are attending your household duties, when you engage in conversation, God is

---

131 White, *The SDA Bible Commentary*, vol. 7, p. 971.
132 *Ibid.* (emphasis added).
133 *Ibid.*
134 White, *Testimonies for the Church*, vol. 5, p. 454.

measuring you. Remember that your words and actions are being daguerreotyped [photographed] in the books of heaven, as the face is reproduced by the artist on the polished plate.[135]

White included an entire chapter on the two witnesses. The topic of the chapter is primarily about the French Revolution, and throughout the chapter, she described the two witnesses. She accepted the Seventh-day Adventist understanding of the time that "the two witnesses represent the Scriptures of the Old and New Testament."[136] As would be expected, she accepted the application of the 42 months/1,260 days to the period of papal domination of Europe during the medieval era:

> The periods here mentioned—"forty and two months," and "a thousand two hundred and threescore days"—are the same, alike representing the time in which the church of Christ was to suffer oppression from Rome. The 1260 years of papal supremacy began in A.D. 538, and would therefore terminate in 1798.[137]

White said this is the period during which the two witnesses would prophesy while "clothed in sackcloth": "when those who dared to proclaim [the Bible's] sacred truths were hunted, betrayed, tortured, buried in dungeon cells, martyred for their faith, or compelled to flee to mountain fastnesses … then the faithful witnesses prophesied in sackcloth."[138] She went on to say that after the witnesses had prophesied in sackcloth, "another power—the beast from the bottomless pit—was to arise to make open, avowed war upon the word of God … This prophecy has received a most exact and striking fulfillment in the history of France during the Revolution."[139]

Finally, Ellen White identified the ascension of the two witnesses to heaven with the establishment of Bible societies following the French Revolution. "Since France made war upon God's two witnesses, they have been honored as never before. In 1804 the British and Foreign Bible Society was organized … In 1816 the American Bible Society was founded."[140]

---

135 White, *The SDA Bible Commentary*, vol. 7, p. 972.
136 White, *The Great Controversy*, p. 267.
137 *Ibid.*, p. 266.
138 *Ibid.*, p. 267.
139 *Ibid.*, p. 269.
140 *Ibid.*, p. 287.

This is a mere summary of the explanation of the two witnesses Ellen White gave. I recommend you read the entire chapter on the two witnesses in The Great Controversy to get her full understanding on this topic.

Now it's time to deal with Ellen White's understanding of the 42 months/1,260 days in Revelation 11:2, 3. This will be the topic of the next chapter.

Chapter 16

What Ellen White Said About Prophetic Time

In the previous chapter, I stated that in my opinion, the 42 months/1,260 days in Revelation 11:1, 2 and the 42 months in Revelation 13:5 represent three-and-a-half years of literal time during the final crisis. I'm sure, had I written this book during Ellen White's lifetime, she would have objected strongly to this interpretation. The reason I say this is she was very straightforward on this topic during the 70 years of her ministry. I did a search on the White Estate website for references to "definite time," "prophetic time," and "prophetic periods," and I'll share with you what I found, beginning with definite time.

Definite Time

Ellen White was *very* emphatic that there is to be no more definite time after 1844. The first question is, What did she mean by "definite time"? The following quote answers that question:

> The preaching of a *definite time for the judgment,* in the giving of the first message, was ordered of God. The computation of the prophetic periods on which that message was based, placing the close of the 2300 days in the autumn of 1844, stands without impeachment.[141]

Clearly, by "definite time," White meant a prophetic period, the end point of which can be calculated prior to its fulfillment. That is evident from what I emphasized in the above quote. Seventh-day Adventists understand that the investigative judgment in heaven began in 1844—more specifically, on October 22.

There are two "definite time" prophecies in Daniel: the 2,300-day prophecy in Daniel 8:14 and the 70-week prophecy in Daniel 9:25. The reason why these are definite time prophecies is that the beginning point

---
141 White, *The Great Controversy*, p. 457 (emphasis added).

is stated very clearly in the latter: *"From the going forth of the command to restore and build Jerusalem until Messiah the Prince, there shall be seven weeks and sixty-two weeks"* (NKJV, emphasis added). Seven weeks plus sixty-two weeks is sixty-nine weeks, which is 483 years with the year-day principle. This period of time began when the emperor Artaxerxes issued his decree for the rebuilding of Jerusalem in 457 B.C. Therefore, the endpoint came 483 years later in A.D. 27.[142] Sure enough, Jesus was baptized that year,[143] marking the beginning of His ministry. And since the 2,300-day prophecy in Daniel 8 shares the same beginning date with the 70-week prophecy in chapter 9, the ending year for the 2,300 days is 1844.

Here is another quote about definite time:

> This time, which the angel [of Revelation 10] declares with a solemn oath, is not the end of this world's history, neither of probationary time, but of prophetic time, which should precede the advent of our Lord. That is, the people will not have another message upon definite time. After this period of time [the 2,300 days/years], reaching from 1842 to 1844, *there can be no definite tracing of the prophetic time.* The longest reckoning reaches to the autumn of 1844.[144]

Therefore, when Ellen White said there are to be no more "definite time" prophecies or "definite tracing of the prophetic time," she meant there will be no more time prophecies with a beginning year that can be known and therefore an ending date that can be calculated in advance of the prophecy's fulfillment. And if that were all she had to say about time prophecies, I would be on fairly safe ground interpreting the 42 months/1,260 days in Revelation 11:2, 3 and the 42 months in 13:5 as literal time still in the future. However, she also spoke about "prophetic time" prophecies and "prophetic period" prophecies. We will now examine those that are most relevant to our discussion in this chapter.

---

142 If you do the simple arithmetic (483-457), you'll come up with A.D. 26. That's because there is no year 0 between 1 B.C. and A.D. 1. Therefore, you have to add a year to 26 to make up for the absence of a year 0.

143 The specific date of October 22 that year was based on the assumption that the event to occur on that day was the Day of Atonement in the Hebrew Karite calendar. It had nothing to do with the date for the restoration and rebuilding of Jerusalem because that specific date is not known. Only the year 457 B.C. is known. Simple arithmetic brings you to 1843, which is why William Miller originally gave 1843 as the year for the end of the 2,300 days and (in his view) the second coming of Christ. However, a year has to be added to 1843 for the same reason it had to be added to 26 for the coming of the Messiah (see the above footnote).

144 White, *The SDA Bible Commentary*, vol. 7, p. 971, (emphasis added).

"Prophetic time" and "prophetic period" prophecies. A search for these terms on the White Estate website makes it very clear that she used these terms primarily in connection with the October 22, 1844 event. However, some of her comments are more general than that. I will share two of them with you. The first one is about prophetic *periods* and the second one is about prophetic *time*:

> "The angel which I saw stand upon the sea and upon the earth lifted up his hand to heaven, and sware by him that liveth forever and ever, who created the heaven, and the things that are therein, and the sea, and the things which are therein, that there should be time no longer (Rev. 10:5, 6)." This message announces *the end of the prophetic periods* The disappointment of those who expected to see our Lord in 1844 was indeed bitter to those who had so ardently looked for His appearing. It was in the Lord's order that the disappointment should come, and that hearts should be revealed.[145]

These words are clearly in the context of the 1844 great Advent movement. Notice that in the following quote, Ellen White used both the terms "prophetic periods" and "prophetic time":

> I saw that [the Millerites] were correct in their reckoning of the *prophetic periods*; *prophetic time* closed in 1844, and Jesus entered the most holy place to cleanse the sanctuary at the ending of the days.[146]

In both of these quotations, the context is the proclamation of the coming of Jesus during the 1844 movement, so it could be argued that Ellen White had in mind the same idea of definite time of which she spoke so often in reference to the end of the 2,300 days in 1844. However, the fact is she said what she said.

The Two Time Periods in Revelation 11:2, 3

In light of these very specific statements by Ellen White about "definite time," "prophetic time," and "prophetic periods," how should we interpret the 42 months/1,260 days in Revelation 11:2, 3? Let's examine each of them. The first one is the time during which the Gentiles (the wicked)

---

[145] White, *Selected Messages*, book 2 (Washington, DC: Review and Herald Publishing Association, 1958), p. 108. (emphasis added).
[146] White, *Early Writings* (Washington, DC: Review and Herald Publishing Association, 1882), p. 243 (emphasis added).

"will trample on the holy city for 42 months" (verse 2), which is the time of the persecution of the two witnesses; and the second one is about the time during which God "will give power to [His] two witnesses, and they will prophecy for 1,260 days, clothed in sackcloth" (verse 3).

"Now when they have finished their testimony …" (verse 7). In a previous chapter, I pointed out that this statement is clearly a reference to the close of probation because the proclamation of the final warning will continue until the close of probation. Therefore, this statement about the two witnesses finishing their testimony will clearly happen at or just before the close of probation. However, there is no indication of a beginning point for the three-and-a-half literal years I have suggested for the 42 months/1,260 days in Revelation 11. Therefore, these two time periods are clearly *indefinite* time.

However, this isn't the end of the argument, because in chapter 13 of this book, I also discussed the 42 months in Revelation 13:5. Here, I believe there is the possibility it could refer to a definite time period. The beast was able to "exercise his authority for 42 months" (verse 5). At this point, this is very indefinite time because there is no indication of when the 42 months will begin or end. However, the beast "was given authority over every tribe, people, language and nation" (verse 7). Keep in mind that during the Middle Ages, the papacy had political authority over the states of Europe, at least insofar as the relationship of the state to the church and the state's enforcement of the church's doctrines was concerned. And the whole point of the first beast in Revelation 13:7 is it will have over authority "over every tribe, people, language and nation." In other words, the beast power will be given *global* authority. While the text doesn't actually *say* this, I think it's reasonable to assume the authority the beast is given in verse 7 is the same authority it is given in verse 5, which will last for 42 months or three-and-a-half years.

With this in mind, we can presumably say at a point in the future, when the papacy is given political authority to enforce its religious dogmas over the entire world, the three-and-a- half literal years of verse 5 will begin, and the ending point should be very easy to determine.

That is *definite* time. And Ellen White said the last *definite* time prophecy ended in 1844. There will be no more definite time after that.

In response, I will mention two things. First, in an Ellen White comment to which I referred earlier in this chapter, she said, "the people will not have another *message* upon definite time," and I can fully agree with that. I would say that what I have shared with you in this entire book is not necessarily a message God will have for us to proclaim to the world. If, at some point in the future, my interpretation of the seven trumpets turns out to be correct, we may *choose* to share our understanding with those outside of our own Seventh-day Adventist faith, but that will not be our *message*; and by all means, the part about the 42 months (three-and-a- half *literal* years) will *not* be our message for the general public. If my interpretation of the 42 months is correct, then I believe the only reason God gave it to us is for the comfort of His people: they can know that the period of their persecution is very limited. It will soon be over.

> *If my interpretation of the 42 months is correct, I believe God gave it to us for the comfort of His people.*

You may say the 42 months in Revelation 11:2 will end with the close of probation and we are not supposed to know when that will happen, and I agree. However, I believe those 42 months are not exactly the same time periods as the 42 months of 13:5. The 42 months of 11:3 have to do with the proclamation of God's end-time message, which will end with the close of probation or perhaps shortly before.

On the other hand, the 42 months of Revelation 13:5 have to do with the global political power of the papacy during the final years of earth's history, and that won't end with the close of probation because the world's persecution of God's people will definitely continue through most of the time of trouble. However, neither will the 42 months conclude with the second coming of Christ because Revelation 17:16 suggests the nations of the world will turn against the papacy *prior* to Christ's second coming: "The beast and the ten horns you saw will hate the prostitute [the papacy]. They will bring her to ruin and leave her naked; they will eat her flesh and burn her with fire."

I now want to remind you of the three reasons why I believe the 42 months of Revelation 13:5 should be understood as literal, all of which I shared with you in an earlier chapter. First is the context of Revelation 12 and 13; second is the time for the healing of the fatal wound; and third is the relationship between the papacy and the United States—that is, the beast from the sea and the beast from the land. Let's take a look at these three reasons.

1. The context between Revelation 12 and Revelation 13. Revelation 12 provides a symbolic synopsis of Christian history, especially the dragon's pursuit of the woman, which was fulfilled by the medieval persecution of God's faithful followers by the Catholic Church. In an effort to destroy the woman, the serpent (i.e., the dragon, or Satan) "spewed water like a river [from his mouth], to overtake the woman and sweep her away with the torrent" (verse 15). This would be the time of the most intense papal persecution of Protestants during a 500-years period, circa 1200–1700. However, "the earth helped the woman by opening its mouth and swallowing the river that the dragon had spewed out of his mouth" (verse 16). Seventh-day Adventists have traditionally interpreted this to refer to the discovery of America and the establishment of freedom of religion by the United States government, and I fully agree with that interpretation.

Then comes verse 17: "the dragon was enraged at the woman and went off to make war against the rest of her offspring—those who obey God's commands and hold to the testimony of Jesus." This is the vicious attack against God's Sabbath-keeping people by the papacy that will take place during the world's final crisis. And then comes Revelation 13, which describes that persecution in great detail, but because of the 42 months in verse 5, we have traditionally backed away from interpreting 13:1–10 as a further description of the enraged dragon's end-time persecution of God's people, interpreting it instead as the persecution of His people between A.D. 538 and 1798. However, I believe the most logical way to understand verses 1–10 is that they are a further description of the enraged dragon's persecution of God's people *during the end time,* that to which we commonly refer as "the final crisis."

The context is my first reason for saying that I believe the 42 months of Revelation 13:5 refer to a literal three-and-a-half years during the world's final crisis.

2. The time for the healing of the fatal wound. "One of the heads of the beast seemed to have had a fatal wound, but the fatal wound *had been healed*" (verse 3, emphasis added). Please note that the healing of the fatal wound takes place *before* the beast is given its 42 months of global authority. And, as I pointed out in a previous chapter, while the healing began with the Lateran Treaty in 1929, the papacy still has not received authority "over every tribe, people, language and nation" (verse 7). Therefore, the wound still has not been fully healed, which means the 42 months still have not begun.

This is my second reason for concluding that the 42 months in Revelation 13:5 have to be interpreted as literal time, because there can't possibly be 1,260 *years* between the healing of the fatal wound and Christ's second coming—or so we fervently hope!

3. The relationship between the two beast powers, the United States and the papacy. Finally, the relationship between the two beast powers of Revelation 13 persuades me to believe the 42 months in verse 5 *have to be literal*. The beast that rises out of the land supports the beast that rises out of the sea in the same way the political powers of Europe supported the papacy during the Middle Ages. The papacy had no military power then to enforce its dogmas on the people of Europe. When the Protestant Reformation broke upon the continent in the early 1500s, the papacy responded viciously, but it had to depend on the various nations of Europe to enforce its hostility on the reformers and their "heretical" teachings. For example, when the church charged Martin Luther with heresy, he didn't appear for trial before a Catholic Church court. He appeared before Charles V, the emperor of the Holy Roman Empire, at the imperial court in Worms, Germany.

It's the same with the land beast in Revelation 13. "It exercised all the authority of the first beast *on his behalf*" (verse 12, emphasis added). The same is true of verse 14: the land beast "deceived the inhabitants of the earth [and] ordered them to set up an image *in honor of the beast who was wounded by the sword and yet lived*" (emphasis added). In both cases, the United States becomes the enforcement arm of the papacy. And, as I pointed out in an earlier chapter, in order for that to happen, the two beasts have to exist *simultaneously*. It would have been impossible for the United States to be the enforcement arm of the papacy during the Middle Ages because it did not exist at that time. The United States came into its infantile existence just as the papacy was dying in its old age. However, then the fatal wound gets healed, and now the papacy needs a new political enforcer. And by the time the papacy needs that new enforcer, the United States has "grown up" to become the world's dominant global superpower. In other words, the United States is now in a position to become the enforcement arm of the papacy.

I will also point out there is a future application of Revelation's prophecy about the deadly wound:

> However, the prophet envisioned a much greater restoration. He saw the wound completely healed, as the Greek implies. Following the healing he saw "all that dwell upon the earth," except the faithful few, worshiping the beast ... *This is still future.* Though the papacy

receives homage from certain groups, vast populations show it no deference. *But that is to change.*[147]

4. *Regarding the papacy's rule* "over all kindreds, and tongues, and nations" (Rev 13:7, KJV):

> This refers to the sphere of [the papacy's] operations, and applies to the heyday of the papacy, perhaps during the Middle Ages, when it exercised almost undisputed sway over Europe ... but especially when, in the future, the power of the papacy will be more fully revived.[148]

These are my reasons for concluding that the time periods of Revelation 11 and 13 have to be understood as literal time, not symbolic time.

My Conclusion

How should you and I relate to all this? I think it's up to each reader to decide how he or she will relate to what I've presented in this book; this applies to my interpretation of both the trumpets as end-time events and, more specifically, to the 42 months/1,260 days of Revelation 11 and 13 as literal rather than symbolic time. I will only say this: Ellen White was a great proponent of taking the Bible as our first and final authority on matters of both doctrine and spiritual life, and I find the biblical evidence for a literal interpretation of the 42 months in Revelation 13:5 to be *very* strong. You read and decide for yourself.

---

[147] Nichol, *The Seventh-day Adventist Bible Commentary*, vol. 7, pp. 817, 818 (emphasis added).
[148] *Ibid.*, p. 819.

Chapter 17

The Seventh Trumpet

The first thing to notice about the seventh trumpet is our vision shifts from events on earth to events transpiring in heaven. We saw in chapter 11 of this book that the sixth trumpet, like all the other trumpets, ends after the close of probation. This means everyone has made their final decision, sealing their destiny for eternity. This is good news for God's people but terrible news for the wicked inhabitants of the world because there is no more hope for them. They are doomed to suffer the fiery glory of God's presence (Heb. 12:29, 2 Thess. 1:8) and eternal separation from Him, the Lifegiver (1 John 5:12). What could be more terrible than that?

I will state my understanding of the seventh trumpet at the beginning of our discussion and then follow up with a more complete explanation. I believe the seventh trumpet gives us a glimpse of a grand ceremony by which heaven's inhabitants will celebrate the soon coming of Christ to this earth. I don't know how many parts this ceremony will actually have, but Revelation gives us tiny segments of three.

The First Segment of the Grand Ceremony: The Loud Voice in Heaven

Please notice the words that open the seventh trumpet: "Loud voices in heaven" proclaim, "The kingdom of the world has become the kingdom of our Lord and of His Christ, and he will reign forever and ever" (Rev. 11:15). I find excellent parallels to this verse in Daniel 7 and Daniel 2:

> [A son of man—Jesus] was given authority, glory and sovereign power; all peoples, nations and people of every language worshiped him. His dominion is an everlasting dominion that will not pass away, and his kingdom is one that will never be destroyed ... Then the sovereignty, power and greatness of the kingdoms under heaven will be handed over to the holy people of the Most High. His

kingdom will be an everlasting kingdom, and all rulers will worship and obey him. (Dan. 7:14, 27)

In the time of those kings the God of heaven will set up a kingdom that will never be destroyed, nor will it be left to another people. It will crush all those kingdoms and bring them to an end, it will itself endure forever. (Dan. 2:44)

Adventists have always understood these verses in Daniel to refer to the second coming of Christ and the establishment of His eternal kingdom. However, the seventh trumpet, which appears to fulfill Daniel's prediction, is not the second coming of Christ. It doesn't show us Jesus' actual descent to the earth on a cloud, as we see in Revelation 6:12–17 and 14:14–20. It doesn't even describe the second coming of Jesus symbolically, as we see in 19:11–16 (Christ and His angels riding out of heaven on white horses). The seventh trumpet takes place entirely *in heaven*. Therefore, I conclude it takes place a short time *before* Christ's actual second coming.

With that said, what do the words, "The kingdom of the world has become the kingdom of our Lord and of his Christ, and he will reign forever and ever" have to do with the second coming of Christ? A great deal, actually. Jesus conquered Satan's kingdom at the cross, but the pre-advent or investigative judgment that began in heaven is, among other things, a great heavenly legal process that has to take place before Jesus can intervene in earth's affairs. His right to rescue the world and its kingdoms from Satan must rest on a solid legal foundation that is recognized as just and right by all the righteous inhabitants of the universe.

> **The seventh trumpet gives us a glimpse of the ceremony, at the conclusion of the judgment, at which Jesus is crowned King.**

The investigative judgment establishes that right beyond any doubt in the minds of the angels and all the other holy beings whom God has created. Daniel made it clear that it is the judgment that gives the kingdoms of the world to Jesus: "But the court will sit, and [the little horn's or Satan's] power *will be taken away and completely destroyed forever*. Then [and not until then] the sovereignty, power and greatness of *all the kingdoms under heaven will be handed over to the holy people* of the Most High" (Dan. 7:26, 27, emphasis added).

According to Daniel, the heavenly court will give the world's kingdoms to Jesus and His people. This is the court's final decision. When that decision is made, the court will be dismissed.

Adventists have always believed the close of probation and the conclusion of the investigative judgment will occur at the same time, and I agree with this concept. The announcement that "the kingdom of the world has become the kingdom of our Lord and of his Christ, and he will reign forever and ever" (Rev. 11:15) is clear evidence that the court has given its final verdict. The investigative judgment is over, and probation has closed. Now Jesus can be crowned King of kings and Lord of lords over all the earth. Now He has a right to return to this earth, allow the destruction of its human kingdoms, and establish His own eternal kingdom of peace. The seventh trumpet gives us a glimpse of the ceremony, at the conclusion of the judgment, at which Jesus is crowned King.

The Second Segment of the Grand Ceremony: The Song of the Twenty-four Elders

The first song was sung by "loud voices in heaven" (Rev. 11:15). The second song is sung by the twenty-four elders. Here is the first part of their song: "And the twenty-four elders, who were seated on their thrones before God, fell on their faces and worshiped God, saying: 'We give thanks to you, Lord God Almighty, the One who is and who was, because you have taken your great power and have begun to reign'" (verses 16, 17).

Verse 15 announced that the court has given the kingdom of the world to God and Christ, and verse 17 announces that God's rulership over the world has already begun: "You *have* taken your great power and *have* begun to reign" (emphasis added). The rest of the twenty-four elders' song supports the conclusion that probation has closed and the end of the world and Christ's second coming are near: "The nations were angry, and your wrath has come. The time has come for judging the dead, and for rewarding your servants the prophets and your people who revere your name, both great and small—and for destroying those who destroy the earth" (verse 18).

The twenty-four elders make several important announcements. The first is that "your wrath has come." The time of God's wrath is the time following the close of probation, when He will pour out the seven last plagues. The wording suggests the time of God's wrath—the time when God withdraws his protection (Rom. 1:18, 26, 28)—has just started. This reinforces the point I've been making: The seventh trumpet comes after the close of probation.

The next important announcement is "The time has come for judging the dead, and for rewarding your servants the prophets" (Rev. 11:18). Jesus has not yet returned to the earth, but the time has come for Him to do so, both to allow the wicked to die and His saints—both living and those raised from the dead—to be taken back to heaven with Him ("rewarding your servants the prophets").

Finally, the twenty-four elders announce that the time has come "for destroying those who destroy the earth" (verse 18). All of these announcements are associated with the second coming of Jesus, which is about to happen!

The Third Segment of the Grand Ceremony: Throwing Open Heaven's Most Holy Place

The seventh trumpet closes with these dramatic words: "Then God's temple in heaven was opened, and within his temple was seen the ark of his covenant. And there came flashes of lightning, rumblings, peals of thunder, an earthquake, and a severe hailstorm" (Rev. 11:19).

This is the closing verse, not only of the seven trumpets but also of the seven churches and seven seals. It's the introduction to the next major section of Revelation, chapters 12–20, which describe quite in detail, albeit symbolically, the final days of the great controversy between Christ and Satan. Revelation 20 concludes with the destruction of Satan and all his evil followers. For this reason, some interpreters of Revelation have suggested 11:19 should actually be the first verse of chapter 12, and I tend to agree with that idea. However, the verse divisions were added much later and weren't inspired. I like the following comment on 11:19:

> [The] ... reason for mentioning of the Ark of the Covenant is to prepare readers for the chapters which concern God's faithfulness to his end-time church. In the Old Testament, the Ark of the Covenant was a symbol of God's continuing presence with His people and the assurance of his promise. As the ark of the covenant was the reminder to Israel of God's loyal love during their wilderness journeys and battles, so the reference to the Ark of the Covenant in Revelation 11:19 is a reminder to God's end-time people of his love and covenant promise to be with them through all the trials

that they will experience in the closing period of earth's history. Whatever trials are to come, God will stay faithful as he promised to carry out "his covenant promises and destroy the enemies of his people"[149]

This brings us to the close of our study of the seven trumpets. We've covered a lot of ground in these pages, and now it's time to bring the various parts together into a unified whole. That will be the topic of the next chapter. This will be followed by a final chapter that shares with you some thoughts about what you and I can do to prepare to remain faithful during that short but most difficult time in human history.

---

149   Stefanovic, pp. 369, 370.

Chapter 18

Putting the Pieces Together

A jigsaw puzzle is made up of many pieces. A child's puzzle may have 10 or 15 pieces while an adult puzzle may have 1,000 or even 3,000 pieces. Fortunately, the person putting the pieces together into a complete picture isn't left totally on his or her own to figure out which pieces should be connected with which other pieces. The puzzle provides a picture, usually on the cover of the box in which the pieces came, that shows what the completed picture will look like when all the pieces are fitted together.

With this said, one can look at the pieces and, for example, find the ones that show sky and clouds, bodies of water, buildings, flowers, animals, etc., and with this, he or she can start creating the picture. It's also easy to find the edge pieces and even easier to find the corner pieces.

I like to think of the seven trumpets as something like a jigsaw puzzle. The complete text in Revelation 8–11 can be compared to the picture on the cover of the jigsaw puzzle, and the individual trumpets, together with the two parts of the interlude, constitute the various pieces. There's one major difference, however, between a jigsaw puzzle and the trumpets: The trumpets don't provide us with an actual picture printed on a box. They are words on the pages of our Bibles. The trumpets do provide us with plenty of images, which is helpful.

The first four trumpets show us (1) hail and fire, (2) a huge mountain, (3) a great star, and (4) the sun, moon, and stars, all falling from the sky and creating havoc on the earth. In the fifth trumpet, we see locusts emerging from an abyss, and the sixth trumpet describes a huge army that kills millions of people. And the fact that all the pieces follow one after another suggests we're looking at a sequence of events in historical time, which, of course, is how Seventh-day Adventists have always interpreted the trumpets.

We have traditionally brought over the historicist method of prophetic interpretation from Daniel's apocalyptic prophecies and applied it to the seven churches, seven seals, and seven trumpets. According to this picture, the symbols in the various segments of the prophecy begin with the first century A.D. and continue in sequence to the time of the end. I agree that the trumpets describe history, but I have adopted a different historical context. My picture is eschatological—end-time events.

These two pictures provide us with two significantly different ways to fit together the pieces of the trumpets. I'll conclude with a chronological overview of these pictures.

The Silence in Heaven

"When he opened the seventh seal, there was silence in heaven for about half an hour" (Rev. 8:1). The traditional Seventh-day Adventist interpretation of this silence is it represents the absence of Jesus and the angels in heaven because they are on their way to earth for His second coming. Other Bible students have understood this silence to represent the awe of the angels as they contemplate what's about to happen, both in heaven and on the earth.[150] Let's consider both reasons for the awe.

Awe over what's about to happen in heaven. In Revelation 8:3–5, an angel, who I believe is Jesus, stands at the altar of incense holding a censer that's filled with incense. This symbolizes Christ's mediatorial ministry in the heavenly sanctuary on behalf of His people and the world.[151] However, He fills His censer with coals from the altar, then hurls it to the earth, causing "peals of thunder, rumblings, flashes of lightning, and an earthquake" (verse 5). I believe this act symbolizes the fact that probation for the world at large has ended, and God's protective hand is removed. This, as I understand it, is the first cause of the awe—the silence—in heaven.

Awe over what's about to happen on the earth. With the removal of God's protective hand, the terrible calamities of the first four trumpets and the release of the demonic forces in the fifth and sixth trumpets can be unleashed upon the world. These calamities and demonic forces are the second cause of the silence in heaven. It's the awe the angels experience as they contemplate what's about to happen on the earth.

---

150 See Nichol, *The Seventh-day Adventist Bible Commentary*, vol. 7, p.787.
151 I'm not suggesting there is a literal altar of incense in the heavenly sanctuary. In the Old Testament sanctuary, the priests ministered daily at the altar of incense (see Exod. 30:1–10). This ministry was a type Christ's "daily" ministry in the heavenly sanctuary.

The Trumpets

In Revelation 8:6, the angels who hold the seven trumpets prepare to sound them. The first six trumpets and the interlude both cover the period of the final crisis. However, the trumpets depict this time from the perspective of the calamities and demonic forces that are unleashed upon the world, while the interlude depicts the same period of time from the perspective of the mission of God's people and the response of the wicked as His people carry out that mission.

The terrible natural disasters of the first four trumpets will come upon the world during the final crisis. When God removes the restraints He has placed on Satan, and allows Satan to demonstrate his rulership style before the universe, these events will convince the world's inhabitants of the cruel, innate malevolence of Satan's character and rulership. However, neither the wicked nor the righteous will change their minds about God.

> *White was emphatic that spiritualism will be rampant and thoroughly explained its nature and its danger during the final crisis.*

This picture of the trumpets fits very nicely with Ellen White's description of the final crisis. She also described terrible natural disasters coming upon the world during this time. She said thousands of cities will be destroyed[152]; "a sudden and unlooked-for calamity ... brings the soul face to face with death"[153]; an "overwhelming surprise" will hit the world at some point in the future.[154] She also spoke about large balls of fire falling on the earth, which agrees with the asteroid concept of the first four trumpets (see the chapter which covers this topic).

Ellen White was also very emphatic that spiritualism will be rampant during the final crisis. She thoroughly explained the nature of spiritualism and its danger for God's people during the end time.[155]

---

152 See White, *Evangelism*, p. 29.
153 White, *Christ's Object Lessons*, p. 412.
154 White, *Testimonies for the Church*, vol. 8, p. 28.
155 See White, *The Great Controversy*, pp. 492–562.

Comparing Chronologies

Now I'd like to compare two chronologies of the seven trumpets.

The traditional view. This view begins with the censer scene, which different sources say represents the close of probation and is still future.[156]

- The first six trumpets back the reader up to the first century A.D. and move forward a trumpet at a time through Christian history to the Great Awakening and the establishment of the Bible societies in the early 1800s.
- The interlude, part 1: In Revelation 10, Jesus declares the conflict between good and evil is almost over, and this is followed by a symbolic representation of the 1844 disappointment and the commission for God's people to proclaim the final warning to the world—a commission Seventh-day Adventists have been carrying out for many decades since 1844.[157]
- The interlude, part 2: In chapter 11, the two witnesses revert back to the first century and move forward through Christian history to the French Revolution in 1790s.
- The seventh trumpet sounds immediately after the close of probation.

An alternate view. This chronological interpretation carries the reader straight through the end time with only one shift in time between the first six trumpets and the interlude:

- The censer scene shows the close of probation for the world at large, which will occur a short time before the final close of probation, just before Christ's second coming.
- The censer scene opens the way for the first four angels to sound their trumpets, which announce terrible natural disasters to fall upon the earth.
- This is followed by trumpets five and six, which describe the release of demonic forces on the earth.
- The interlude carries the reader back to the beginning of the trumpets period and depicts the mission of God's people during that period of time.

---

156 See Smith, p. 474; Nichol, *The Seventh-day Adventist Bible Commentary*, vol. 7, p. 787.
157 It's important to understand Protestants of many other denominations have also been winning souls to Christ all over the world since 1844, but with a general Christian message, not the unique Seventh-day Adventist message.

- The seventh trumpet follows the final gospel proclamation by the two witnesses.

This is the "big picture" of both views.

This brings us to the end of our discussion of the seven trumpets. This means that God's people today are facing a terrible crisis for which we need to be prepared, especially spiritually. We need to be developing our relationship with God. We need, more than ever, the outpouring of the Holy Spirit—the latter rain—into our minds and hearts so that we will be prepared to endure the trials of the final crisis and fulfill the mission of the two witnesses with Spirit-filled power. This spiritual preparation will be part of the focus of the final chapter.

Chapter 19

Getting Ready for the Events of the Trumpets

One of the humorous side effects of the coronavirus pandemic that hit the world in early 2020 is the toilet paper panic. People grabbed them off the shelves of stores by the armloads. I can remember going to Walmart, Walgreens, Costco, and other local grocery stores in search of toilet paper and couldn't find any. Facial tissues, hand sanitizer wipes, and alcohol-based disinfectant were equally impossible to find. But why? The sanitizer and hand wipes I could sort of understand, because they help to remove germs from our hands and the things we touch. But toilet paper? What on earth does *that* have to do with the coronavirus pandemic? A lot, when you understand the craziness of human psychology. Think of the phrase "toilet paper panic." The word "panic" means "profound fear," and profound fear can drive us to do strange things.

Now let me remind you of a passage I shared with you earlier in this book:

> There will be signs in the sun, moon and stars. On the earth, nations will be in anguish and perplexity at the roaring and tossing of the sea. People will faint from terror, apprehensive of what is coming on the world, for the heavenly bodies will be shaken. (Luke 21:25, 26)

Please pay careful attention to these words: "anguish," "perplexity," and "terror." Another word that describes what Luke wrote is "panic." When the calamities of the end time begin, whether they pertain to the seven trumpets or are the ones about which Ellen White wrote, I can assure you "panic" will be the operative word. And it won't just be individual citizens grabbing toilet paper off the shelves of Costco and Walgreens. It will also be governments all over the world. Luke said, "*nations* will be in anguish and perplexity." Let me remind you of a quote I shared with you in the chapter on the sixth trumpet:

> In [times of] crisis [panic] we allow people to take over and enact unusual procedures. Crisis feeds on the illusion that control can bring the situation under control. Crisis are used to excuse drastic and erratic action on the part of managers ... Individuals have fewer responsibilities in crisis *as management gathers power to ride out the problem. When crisis is the norm, management tends to assume an unhealthy amount of power on a daily basis.*[158]

From the beginning of our movement, Adventists have warned that Revelation 13 will bring about just that kind of reaction: the two beasts assuming an unhealthy amount of power over the entire human population. Think of the world's reaction to the 9/11 crisis. Airports all over the world enforced the screening of passengers before they would be allowed to board airplanes. This was a huge invasion of people's personal privacy, but the fear of terrorists caused everyone to accept it as something that *had* to be done in order to protect them from the terrorists. And during the world's final crisis, the fear of an angry God will make people willing to give up their religious freedom. Revelation 13 doesn't inform us about the circumstances that will prompt the world's leaders to violate people's freedom of religion and speech, but the first four trumpets do.

> **Think of the world's reaction to the 9/11 crisis. During the final crisis, fear will make people willing to give up their religious freedom.**

Now think of all this in the context of our Adventist understanding of the final crisis. If fear of the coronavirus pandemic caused people to lose their sanity and gobble up toilet paper like crazy, what do you think will be their response to calamities of the end time, both those described in the seven trumpets and those foretold by Ellen White? If toilet paper disappeared from store shelves during the coronavirus pandemic, how will people react when the grocery stores run out of food because of the disruption of both farming, by dark days, and the world's transportation systems that deliver to grocery stores what little food still exists? Suddenly, governments all over the world will impose laws that restrict all kinds of freedom, including freedom of religion. The persecution of dissenters will

---

[158] Anne Wilson Schaef and Diane Fassel, *The Addictive Organization* (New York: HarperCollins Publishers, 1988), p. 160 (emphasis added).

be rampant. God's people will be confronted with the fear of both natural disasters and the ridicule and persecution over their religious convictions.

The question is, How will you and I deal with this situation? I can assure you of one thing: The people who deal most successfully with this fear will be those who are prepared for it. And that preparation takes time because it will be based on our relationship with Jesus, which takes time to develop. Another way to explain it is those who make it through that time on God's side will be those who have learned to depend on Him and overcome the character defects that would cause them to yield their faith.

Demonic spirits will also make their appearance at that time, persuading the world that these calamities are the result of people abandoning their religions. Multitudes will flock back to their false religions and accept the notion that the removal of the religious freedom of a few "dissidents" is justified in order to care for the common good of the human race as a whole.

This is the scenario with which you and I will be confronted in the not-too-distant future. And the question is, How can we prepare for it so we won't succumb to the panic of the disasters and pressure of popular opinion on how to deal with it? That's the theme of this final chapter of my book.

You and I will need four kinds of preparation for that time: physical, mental, character, and spiritual. Let's talk about physical preparation first.

1. Physical Preparation

Very early in our experience as a church, God gave Seventh-day Adventists a message about healthful living that has been a tremendous blessing to those of us who have followed it. I am convinced that one of the primary reasons God gave us this message is to prepare us for the final crisis through which we will have to pass before Jesus comes.

During 2020, I followed a daily devotional book, and the topic for May was physical and mental development. I'd like to share with you some of the highlights I underlined as I went through the month:

> Whatever promotes physical health promotes the development of a strong mind and a well-balanced character. Without health, no one can as distinctly understand or as completely fulfill his obligations to himself, to his fellow beings, or to His Creator. Therefore the health should be as faithfully guarded as the character.[159]

---
159 White, *Reflecting Christ*, p. 137.

We are to beware lest that which is taken into the stomach shall banish from the mind high and holy thoughts.[160]

Anything that lessens physical strength enfeebles the mind and makes it less capable of discriminating between right and wrong. We become less capable of choosing the good and have less strength of will to do that which we know to be right.[161]

It is impossible for the brain to do its best work when the digestive powers are abused.[162]

If you want to prepare well physically for whatever trail lies before you in life—if you want to be prepared for the events announced by the seven trumpets—then one of the best things you can do is practice healthful living.

The major components of this way of life are diet, exercise, water, rest, fresh air, sunlight, and a close relationship with God.[163]

I urge you to seek God's help in becoming aware of the changes you might need to make regarding food, exercise, or any other aspect of physical preparation, so that you will be ready for the events of the trumpets whenever they occur. Paul clarified it this way in 1 Corinthians 6: "Do you not know that your bodies are temples of the Holy Spirit, who is in you, whom you have received from God? You are not your own; you were bought with a price. Therefore honor God with your body" (verses 19, 20).

Being physically well, along with having a mind submitted to the Holy Spirit, will lead to mental and character development.

2. Mental Preparation

Mental preparation must include thorough and correct understanding of Scripture, since Scripture is the entire basis of what keeps us safe. Of course, this will cause us to carry out the scriptural principles we learn from the Bible. For now, let's just talk about mental preparation based on one of John's visions, in Revelation 7:2, 3, which says:

> Then I saw another angel coming up from the east, having the seal of the living God. He called out in a loud voice to the four angels

---

160 Ibid., p. 138.
161 Ibid., p. 140.
162 Ibid., p. 152.
163 These elements are taken from Ellen White, *The Ministry of Healing* (Mountain View, CA: Pacific Press Publishing Association, 1905), p. 127.

who had been given power to harm the land and the sea: "Do not harm the land or the sea or the trees until we put a seal on the foreheads of the servants of our God.'"

This is to say, we must understand the logic and principles found in God's Word.

The frontal lobe of the brain is located behind the forehead: the place where we do our critical thinking and decision making. So it is no surprise to read that "the people of God are sealed in their foreheads—it is not any seal or mark that can be seen, but a settling into the truth, both intellectually and spiritually, so they cannot be moved ...."[164]

What we read, what we watch on TV, DVDs—*whatever we allow to enter our minds*—feeds into mental preparation. We need to be very intentional in guarding our minds against the many clever distractions that Satan designs to trap us into filling our minds with unholy or unkind thoughts. The words of The Lord's Prayer, "lead us not into temptation," must include us doing our part to guard well our thoughts.

3. Character Development

Profound crises are in the near future for all of us. Therefore, one of the most important preparations we can make is character development.

What is "character"? It is who we are when no one sees us—who we are in the dark. Character is our response to the irksome challenges that sneak into our lives, like when we are held up in a traffic jam and use the time in prayer praising or God rather than fuming and fussing. We develop our character when we allow God to convict us about an ugly thought or unkind words that we shouldn't utter or even think.

All of us have character defects of which we are unaware, such as pride, anger, jealousy, guilt, shame, an obsession with money, or anything else that we turn over in our minds again and again. Some of us find it very easy to feel and express anger or frustration. Others are especially controlled by fear. Life can go on fairly smoothly when times are easy but in a crisis, these character defects can control our minds and emotions and cause us to make very unhealthy decisions. How, then can we truly overcome these character defects?

We need to ask God to guide us to an awareness of these so that we can deal with them. Our efforts to obey *without* the power of the Holy

---
164 Ellen White, quoted in Nichol, *The Seventh-day Adventist Bible Commentary*, vol. 4, p. 1161.

Spirit in our minds and hearts is definitely righteousness by works. But our personal effort *when combined* with the power of the Holy Spirit is a critical part of what it means to develop our character *and* to prepare for the crisis ahead.

Victory won't necessarily come easily, but keep in mind that trials are one of the most frequent ways God uses both to make us aware of our character defects and to help us overcome them. Of course, we don't like trials, and we try our best to avoid them. It's so easy to moan and groan about our trials and blame God for them, but the apostle James advised us to "consider it pure joy, my brothers, whenever you face trials of many kinds, because you know that the testing of your faith produces perseverance. Let perseverance finish its work so that you may be mature and complete, not lacking anything" (James 1:2-4). And Ellen White pointed out that "afflictions, crosses, temptations, adversity, and our varied trials *are God's workmen* to refine us, sanctify us and fit us for the heavenly garner."[165]

You will experience ups and downs—successes and failures. That's why you need the assurance provided by the Holy Spirit. When you slip and fall, you can get up and keep on going in full confidence that God isn't sitting up in heaven condemning you. He's applauding your effort! And we have the assurance that when we confess our failure and seek God's forgiveness, He will blot out our sins like a thick cloud (Isa. 44:22, KJV), putting them as far as the east is from the west (Ps. 103:12) and in the depths of the sea (Micah 7:19), and forgetting all about them (Jer. 31:34). John tells us that if we believe on the name of the Son of God, we will *know* that we have eternal life (1 John 5:11-13).

As time goes on, you will recognize that you're making progress, and progress is what you're pursuing, not perfection. That's experimental religion! That's character development.

Also keep in mind that Satan will oppose you at every step. You're dealing with an adversary who won't give up. He will try to discourage you, especially through your failures. We've all heard of a person who threw away their cigarettes and never smoked again, but for every person like that, there are probably a hundred more who struggled for a year, five years, or longer before they conquered that habit. Character development is tough, but with God's help and our persistence in *seeking* help

---

165 White, *Testimonies for the Church*, vol. 3 (Mountain View, CA: Pacific Press Publishing Association, 1875), p. 115, emphasis added.

from God and His Holy Spirit, you will make progress ... you can be even tougher:

> Christ has given us no assurance that to attain perfection of character is an easy matter. A noble, all-round character ... is earned by individual effort through the merits and grace of Christ. [...] It is formed by hard, stern battles with self.[166]

And praying for God to work in us in becoming victorious focuses us on *our* part. For *His* part, God gives us the desire to replace bad habits with good ones and the strength to follow through.

Perfection doesn't happen immediately, but God guarantees that He will get us where we need to be. All the glory goes to God, because with our consent, He does all the heavy lifting! "May God himself, the God of peace, sanctify you through and through. May your whole spirit, soul and body be kept blameless at the coming of our Lord Jesus Christ. The one who calls you is faithful, and he will do it" (1 Thess. 5:23, 24).

You might think that prayer and Bible study are all that are needed to develop character, and that any effort we put forth to develop a righteous character is righteousness by works. However, nothing could be further from the truth. Paul made this utterly clear in his letter to the church in Ephesus.

He began by pointing out that our works count for nothing toward our *salvation*. Instead, he said, "It is by grace you have been saved through faith—and this is not from yourselves. It is the gift of God—*not by works*" (Eph. 2:8, 9, emphasis added). Then he clarified in the very next verse: "For we are God's handiwork, created in Christ Jesus *to do good works*, which God prepared in advance for us to do" (verse 10, emphasis added).

Another aspect of character development is sharing with others what we know and Who we know. The Holy Spirit will guide you in this process each day, and you may find yourself doing wonderful things you hadn't done before. He may give you encouraging words to speak to a coworker or family member. You may find yourself drawn to volunteer somewhere you never had an interest in before. Maybe He will bring you into contact with someone who wants to study the Bible or who wants prayer. You may be led to help someone with physical needs, encouraging them and praying with them and for them.

---

[166] White, *Christ's Object Lessons*, p. 331.

Sharing Jesus and His gospel will propel us forward significantly. Our various ministries, and witnessing to God's character by treating people with love and respect, demonstrate character development.

From the pen of inspiration, we read that "strength to resist evil is best gained by aggressive service."[167] And again, "Some will depart from the faith, giving heed to seducing spirits and doctrines of devils. Why? Because they failed to work diligently."[168] However,

> If we consent, He will so identify Himself with our thoughts and aims, so blend our hearts and minds into conformity to His will, that when obeying Him we shall be but carrying out our own impulses …. When we know God as it is our privilege to know Him, our life will be a life of continual obedience. Through an appreciation of the character of Christ, through communion with God, sin will become hateful to us.[169]

Again, from Thessalonians: "It is God's will that you should be sanctified …" (1 Thess. 4:3a). And Ellen White says,

> None are living Christians unless they have a daily experience in the things of God and daily practice self-denial, cheerfully bearing the cross and following Christ. Every living Christian will advance daily in the divine life.[170]

A Personal Experience

Allow me to share a personal experience. In early June 2014, I experienced profound anxiety. It wasn't anxiety about a specific problem in my life. There was no particular reason for it. It was just anxiety. I sought the help of several psychologists, but none of them were able to provide me with any relief.[171] However, I can tell you what *did* work. What finally brought me relief from this extreme anxiety was my relationship with God.

---

167 White, *Acts of the Apostles*, p. 105.
168 White, *Manuscript Releases*, vol. 1 (Silver Spring, MD: Ellen G. White Estate, 1981), p. 102.
169 White, *The Desire of Ages*. Mountain View, CA: Pacific Press Publishing Association, 1898, p. 668.
170 White, *Testimonies for the Church*, vol. 2, p. 505. White goes on to make the point that failing to meditate and pray daily will result in a decline of religious interest.
171 I don't mean to suggest psychological and psychiatric counseling aren't helpful. They can be very helpful. In my early twenties, I experienced significant depression and sought the help of a Christian psychiatrist who was very helpful. If you are experiencing anxiety, depression, or some other negative psychological problem, I encourage you to try psychological counseling. Ask God to lead you to the person(s) who can be the most helpful in your situation.

When the problem first began, I said, "God, I know that this anxiety isn't going to go away immediately. I know it's going to take time. I ask you to guide me out of it." It took a little over five years, and during that time, I sometimes wondered if I would ever overcome this anxiety, but I persisted in my requests for God to lead me out of it, and He did. The last time I had a severe anxiety attack was in August 2019.

Since that time, I occasionally sense mild anxiety and immediately ask God to help me deal with it, and He does. It may last a few hours or even a day or two, but then I return to normal, healthy feeling and thinking. And with God's help, I'm increasingly able to make a firm choice to have a positive, optimistic attitude—and live that choice.

I have come to realize this anxiety was a character defect I needed to overcome. It was a trial God allowed me to experience so I could be better prepared to deal with whatever difficulties may come in the future. I didn't enjoy the anxiety—far from it! And I wouldn't want to go through those five years again. However, I'm thankful God allowed me to experience this trial because it's made me a better, stronger Christian.

> *I wouldn't want to go through those five years again. However, I'm thankful God allowed me to experience this trial*

In fact, now I sometimes ask God to bring more trials into my life so I can grow and mature in my Christian experience. And guess what: He does! He seems to pile them on! When a new trial pops up in my life, I at first moan and groan a bit, but then I realize, "Oh! This is another of God's trials to help me be a more mature person. Thank You, God! Guide me through it."

There's one other tremendous benefit I've gained through this battle with anxiety and others that have come up since then. They have all deepened my relationship with God. I have learned to sense His presence in my life and trust Him with my future. I used to worry a lot about the future, which was a contributing factor to my anxiety, but I've learned that trusting my future with Him brings a great sense of peace.

"The great work of life is character building."[172] Therefore, set out to be very purposeful about recognizing your character defects and overcoming

---

172 White, *Christian Education*, p. 64.

them. With God's help you *will* succeed—not all at once but in small steps, one day at a time.

In summary, character growth is like physical growth and development. It requires daily "eating" (studying Scripture), "breathing" (prayer), and "moving" (sharing Jesus' love with people with whom we're in contact).

4. Spiritual Preparation for the End Times

This is doubtless the most important part of getting ready for the end times, but it is so intertwined with physical, mental, and character preparation that all of them are actually required to be ready. Without a healthy body (physical preparation), a healthy brain (mental preparation), and a healthy character, one cannot progress spiritually. Spiritual readiness for end-time events is not optional, but essential to every Christian.

Spiritual readiness is defined simply as being in harmony with God every day; trusting God for guidance throughout the day and living by His principles. It encompasses one's personal relationship with God and the resultant changes He makes in our characters.

When we take the oath of loyalty to God (baptism), to remain in effect, this vow must be lived out in life every day by (a) committing to Him in the morning, (b) communicating with Him throughout the day, and (c) diligently studying the Bible. These three steps are crucial in preparing for the end times.

a. Committing to God Upon Awakening

Giving our lives to God first thing in the morning sets the tone for our day. David said, "I am at rest in God alone; my salvation comes from him" (Ps. 62:1, CSB) and "I have set the Lord always before me" (Ps. 16:8, KJV). As Ellen White said:

> Consecrate yourself to God in the morning; make this your very first work. Let your prayer be, "Take me, O Lord, as wholly Thine. I lay all my plans at thy feet. Use me today in Thy service. Abide with me, and let all my work be wrought in Thee." This is a daily matter. Each morning consecrate yourself to God for that day. Surrender all your plans to Him, to be carried out or given up as His providence shall indicate.[173]

---

173 White, *Steps to Christ*, p. 70.

And Jesus tells us, "Remain in me, as I also remain in you …. If you remain in me and I in you, you will bear much fruit …" (John 15:4, 5).

b. *Communicating with God Throughout the Day*

Trusting someone is a function of two things. First, the person you're learning to trust must in fact *be* absolutely, one hundred percent trustworthy—and God is just that. Second, *you* must get to know Him more and more, and the better you know Him, the more you will automatically trust Him.

The question is, how do you get to know God? Getting to know God involves the same process as getting to know a human individual: you talk to them, listen to them, and do things together with them. That's it! Pretty simple, right?

Translating this to the spiritual realm, we pray to God (talking), we read the Bible (listening to God), and we do things together with Him. After our personal daily devotional time with God—praying to Him and reading His Word—we commit our day to God and take with us, all day, an awareness of His presence. After all, He did say, "Never will I leave you; never will I forsake you" (Heb. 13:5).

Throughout the day we continue to communicate with Him. We thank Him when good things happen, ask Him for wisdom if a problem arises, seek His help in resisting temptation, and ask Him for just the right words if we have to deliver difficult information. It's just like Jesus described in John 15:4.

The second part of trusting God more and more is simply living by His principles. So often we tell a half-truth, speak cutting words, or in other ways fall short of living by His principles. So we confess the moment we've erred. We don't save up all the bad things and ask for forgiveness that evening. That's too much of a burden for anyone to bear! We ask for forgiveness right away, which God immediately gives (1 John 1:9), then ask for strength and wisdom so that if the temptation comes again, we can call out for help and not repeat the mistake (see also Phil. 4:13 and 1:6).

We are always covered by Christ's grace. That is to say, we do not lose our salvation when we sin (1 John 5:11-14). We just get back up and try to keep our awareness of Jesus' presence all day long. Out of this daily trust relationship grow spiritual progress and undreamed-of victories! And God has promised that if we keep up this close daily relationship, He will take care of our character needs and have us ready for the end of time: "May God himself, the God of peace, sanctify you through and through. May your whole spirit, soul and body be kept blameless at the coming of our Lord Jesus Christ. The one who calls you is faithful, and he will do it" (1 Thess. 5:23, 24; see also Phil. 1:6).

Do you see that character development is a natural result of your daily personal relationship with God? This daily walk with God is not the air conditioning or window controls of the car—it's the engine. This daily walk with God is not the whipped cream on the pie—it's the pie. So once again:

> Consecrate yourself to God in the morning; make this your very first work. Let your prayer be, "Take me, O Lord, as wholly Thine. I lay all my plans at thy feet. Use me today in Thy service. Abide with me, and let all my work be wrought in Thee." This is a daily matter. Each morning consecrate yourself to God for that day. Surrender all your plans to Him, to be carried out or given up as His providence shall indicate. Thus day by day you may be giving your life into the hands of God, and thus your life will be molded more and more after the life of Christ.[174]

And let us bear in mind these words of caution:

> It is not safe for one day to neglect putting on the Lord Jesus Christ.[175]

> When we permit our communion with God to be broken, our defense is departed from us. Not all your good purposes and good intentions will enable you to withstand evil. You must be men and women of prayer. Your petitions must not be faint, occasional, and fitful, but earnest, persevering, and constant. It is not always necessary to bow upon your knees in order to pray. Cultivate the habit of talking with the Saviour when you are alone, when you are walking, and when you are busy with your daily labor. Let the heart be continually uplifted in silent petition for help, for light, for strength, for knowledge. Let every breath be a prayer.[176]

Paul refers to this in 1 Thessalonians 5:17, where he says, "Pray continually."

Communicating with God means a two-way dialogue. Not only do we talk with Him; He talks with us! He speaks to us in His Word, the Bible, and so along with committing to Him in the morning, we also spend time

---

174 White, *Steps to Christ*, p. 70.
175 White, *Manuscript Releases*, vol. 8 (Silver Spring, MD: Ellen G. White Estate, 1990), p. 10.
176 White, *The Ministry of Healing*, p. 510.

in His Word on a daily basis. Said Job, "I have treasured the words of his mouth more than my daily bread" (Job 23:12). And Jesus said, "It is written: 'Man shall not live on bread alone, but on every word that comes from the mouth of God'" (Matt. 4:4).

> The word of the living God is not merely written, but spoken. The Bible is God's voice speaking to us, just as surely as though we could hear it with our ears. If we realized this, with what awe would we open God's word, and with what earnestness would we search its precepts! The reading and contemplation of the Scriptures would be regarded as an audience with the Infinite One.[177]

Summarizing, we commit to God as we begin our day, praying for enlightenment before reading the Bible. After we've read from His Word, we ask for God's presence during the rest of the day and take the awareness of His presence with us for all the remaining activities of the day. This act of beholding and admiring God all day gives Him the chance to change our characters, which He does! We saw how this works earlier, when we talked about character development.

c. Diligent Bible Study

The third "essential" in spiritual development is Bible study. Know what you believe, and be able to substantiate it from the Bible. Spiritual development requires daily study of the Scriptures. Memorizing Scriptures will fortify your mind and prepare you to be able to resist the devil's temptations and snares:

> All whom God has blessed with reasoning powers are to become intellectual Christians. They are not requested to believe without evidence; therefore Jesus has enjoined upon all to search the Scriptures. Let the ingenious inquirer, and the one who would know for himself what is truth, exert his mental powers to search out the truth as it is in Jesus. Any neglect here is at the peril of the soul. We must know individually the prescribed conditions of entering into eternal life. We must know what is the voice of God, that we may live by every word that proceeds out of his mouth. We cannot allow these questions to be settled for us by another's mind, or another's judgment. We must search the Scriptures carefully with a heart

---

177 White, *Testimonies for the Church*, vol. 6, p. 393.

open to the reception of light and the evidences of truth. We cannot trust the salvation of our souls to ministers, to idle traditions, to human authorities, or to pretensions. We must know for ourselves what God has said. We are laborers together with God, and we want to know, and must know, what conditions are resting upon those who are to be heirs of salvation, or we shall die in our sins. It is not to be our study as to what may be the opinion of men, or of popular faith, or what the Fathers have said. We cannot trust to the voice of the multitude, but we want to know what is the voice of God, what is his revealed will. He has left us his own statements, and we must search for the truth as for hidden treasures. We must put away all skepticism, all exaltation of our own ideas. We must humble our hearts by repentance and with contrition of soul, praying for true enlightenment. We must be diligent and thoughtful. We must be constant learners in the school of Christ, then we shall be meek and lowly of heart as was our Saviour. The Lord positively demands of every Christian an intelligent knowledge of the Scriptures. He must dig for the truth as he would dig for hid treasures. He must search the Scriptures, comparing scripture with scripture; for he must be a laborer together with God. Individually, we are to work out our own salvation with fear and trembling. It is God who works in us, and by us, and through us. God's word is the sword of the Spirit, and with a knowledge of revealed truth, which is our spiritual weapon ....[178]

One more thing before you close this book. Thank you for taking this journey with me. I want above all else to meet you in heaven. I appeal to you today, right now, to stop and pray a prayer of dedication or rededication to God. Choose a daily time when you reconnect with Him and fellowship with Him in Bible reading and prayer.

I look forward to meeting you in heaven—a place where our joy cannot be described and where we can fellowship with one another and with God forever and ever. See you there.

---

178 Ellen White, "Co-Laborers with Christ," The Review and Herald, Mar. 8, 1887.

APPENDIX A

End-Time Disasters Are Allowed by God, but Caused by Satan

The wrath of God is being revealed from heaven against all the godlessness and wickedness of people, who suppress the truth by their wickedness. (Rom. 1:18)

Therefore God gave them over in the sinful desires of their hearts to sexual impurity for the degrading of their bodies with one another. (Rom. 1:24)

Because of this, God gave them over to shameful lusts. Even their women exchanged natural sexual relations for unnatural ones. (Rom. 1:26)

Furthermore, just as they did not think it worthwhile to retain the knowledge of God, so God gave them over to a depraved mind, so that they do what ought not to be done. (Rom. 1:28)

Through spiritualism, Satan appears as a benefactor of the race, healing the diseases of the people, and professing to present a new and more exalted system of religious faith; but at the same time he works as a destroyer. His temptations are leading multitudes to ruin. Intemperance dethrones reason; sensual indulgence, strife, and bloodshed follow. Satan delights in war, for it excites the worst passions of the soul and then sweeps into eternity its victims steeped in vice and blood. It is his object to incite the nations to war against one another, for he can thus divert the minds of the people from the work of preparation to stand in the day of God.

Satan works through the elements also to garner his harvest of unprepared souls. He has studied the secrets of the laboratories of nature, and he uses all his power to control the elements as far as God allows. When he was suffered to afflict Job, how quickly flocks and herds, servants, houses, children, were swept away, one trouble succeeding another as in a moment. It is God that shields His creatures and hedges them in from the power of the destroyer. But the Christian world have shown contempt for the law of Jehovah; and the Lord will do just what He has declared that He would—He will withdraw His blessings from the earth and remove His protecting care from those who are rebelling against His law and teaching and forcing others to do the same. Satan has control of all whom God does not especially guard. He will favor and prosper some in order to further his own designs, and he will bring trouble upon others and lead men to believe that it is God who is afflicting them.

While appearing to the children of men as a great physician who can heal all their maladies, he will bring disease and disaster, until populous cities are reduced to ruin and desolation. Even now he is at work. In accidents and calamities by sea and by land, in great conflagrations, in fierce tornadoes and terrific hailstorms, in tempests, floods, cyclones, tidal waves, and earthquakes, in every place and in a thousand forms, Satan is exercising his power. He sweeps away the ripening harvest, and famine and distress follow. He imparts to the air a deadly taint, and thousands perish by the pestilence. These visitations are to become more and more frequent and disastrous. Destruction will be upon both man and beast. "The earth mourneth and fadeth away," "the haughty people ... do languish. The earth also is defiled under the inhabitants thereof; because they have transgressed the laws, changed the ordinance, broken the everlasting covenant." Isaiah 24:4, 5.

And then the great deceiver will persuade men that those who serve God are causing these evils. The class that have provoked the displeasure of Heaven will charge all their troubles upon those whose obedience to God's commandments is a perpetual reproof to transgressors. It will be declared that men are offending God by the violation of the Sunday sabbath; that this sin has brought calamities which will not cease until Sunday observance shall be strictly enforced; and that those who present the claims of the fourth commandment, thus destroying reverence for Sunday, are troublers of the people, preventing their restoration to divine favor and temporal prosperity. Thus the accusation urged of old against the servant of God will be repeated and upon grounds equally well established: "And it

End-Time Disasters Are Allowed by God, but Caused by Satan

came to pass, when Ahab saw Elijah, that Ahab said unto him, Art thou he that troubleth Israel? And he answered, I have not troubled Israel; but thou, and thy father's house, in that ye have forsaken the commandments of the Lord, and thou hast followed Baalim." 1 Kings 18:17, 18. As the wrath of the people shall be excited by false charges, they will pursue a course toward God's ambassadors very similar to that which apostate Israel pursued toward Elijah.

The miracle-working power manifested through spiritualism will exert its influence against those who choose to obey God rather than men. Communications from the spirits will declare that God has sent them to convince the rejecters of Sunday of their error, affirming that the laws of the land should be obeyed as the law of God. They will lament the great wickedness in the world and second the testimony of religious teachers that the degraded state of morals is caused by the desecration of Sunday. Great will be the indignation excited against all who refuse to accept their testimony.[179]

They had as king over them the angel of the Abyss, whose name in Hebrew is Abaddon and in Greek is Apollyon (that is, Destroyer). (Rev. 9:11)

You belong to your father, the devil, and you want to carry out your father's desires. He was a murderer from the beginning, not holding to the truth, for there is no truth in him. When he lies, he speaks his native language, for he is a liar and the father of lies. (John 8:44)

---

179 White, *The Great Controversy*, pp. 589, 590.

APPENDIX B

Is the Land Beast the United States? (Rev. 13:11)

I will share with you four reasons for identifying the land beast as the United States.

1. ***The land beast is a beast.*** To say the land beast is a beast seems too obvious to be worth mentioning. However, keep in mind that in apocalyptic prophecy, a beast represents a political entity—a nation (for examples, see Dan. 8:20, 21 and Dan. 7:17). The United States is a nation, so it fulfills that specification of the prophecy about the land beast. However, there are many other nations in the world, any one of which could be symbolized by a beast, so we need more than the fact that the United States is a nation to identify it as the land beast in Revelation 13.

2. ***The land beast is an end-time power.*** As far as I know, all interpreters of Revelation 13 understand the mark of the beast to be an end-time phenomenon, which means the beast that enforces the mark is an end-time nation. We live in the time of the end, so the United States qualifies for this characteristic, but so do India, Iran, Nigeria, and every other nation on the planet. Therefore, we need more than the fact that the United States is an end-time nation.

3. ***The land beast is a Christian nation.*** The land beast has "two horns *like a lamb*" (Rev. 13:11, emphasis added). The word "lamb" occurs 31 times throughout Revelation, and in each instance except this one, it is a symbol of Christ, "the lamb of God" (John 1:29). And the United States is a Christian nation. However, so are Germany, Argentina, and Canada, among many others. Therefore, we need more than the fact that the United States is a Christian nation.

4. ***The land beast has global authority.*** Revelation says the beast that rose from the land will make "the earth and its inhabitants worship the first

beast" (Rev. 13:12). It will also cause the nations of the earth "to set up an image in honor of the beast who was wounded by the sword and yet lived" (verse 14). Clearly, this beast is a global superpower, and ever since the end of World War II, the United States has been a global superpower.

When we put all four of these characteristics of the land beast together, the United States is the only one that meets all the conditions:

- The United States is a nation in the world
- The United States is an end-time nation
- The United States is a Christian nation
- The United States is the world's dominant global superpower[180]

This is the reason why I believe the beast that rises out of the earth is the United States of America. No other nation in today's world meets all of these specifications.

---

180 As of 2020, when I wrote this book, Russia and China were both powerful nations that were contending to become the world's only superpower, but the United States still retains that honor.

APPENDIX C

The Seal of God

Here's just a brief synopsis of God's seal.

Those who daily commit their lives to God through prayer and Bible study will receive the seal of God referred to in Revelation 7:3.

"Those who receive the seal of the living God and are protected in the time of trouble must reflect the image of Jesus fully."[181] Remember that this will automatically take place in the context of my daily private time and walk with God (reread John 15:4, 5).

"[T]he people of God are sealed in their foreheads—it is not any seal or mark that can be seen, but a settling into the truth, both intellectually and spiritually, so they cannot be moved...."[182]

"[T]he Sabbath of the fourth commandment is the seal of the living God."[183]

In short, we see that the seal of God is:

A mark (Rev. 7:2, 3)

A sign of permanence or unchangeability (Jer. 32:14)

Given by the Holy Spirit (Eph. 1:13, 4:30)

In the forehead (frontal lobe of the brain, center of thoughts and decision-making; Ezek. 9:4)

An indicator that their thoughts center on God (Isa. 26:3)

Given to those who keep God's commandments (Rev. 14:12, Heb. 8:10)

Also an indicator that they worship God every seventh day, as designated in the fourth commandment, which is the only commandment bearing the seal of God—His name, His territory, and His right to rule (Ex. 20:8-11)

---

181 White, *Early Writings*, p. 71.
182 White, quoted in Nichol, *The Seventh-day Adventist Bible Commentary*, vol. 4, p. 1161.
183 White, *The Great Controversy*, p. 640.

TEACH Services, Inc.
P U B L I S H I N G

We invite you to view the complete
selection of titles we publish at:
www.TEACHServices.com

We encourage you to write us
with your thoughts about this,
or any other book we publish at:
info@TEACHServices.com

TEACH Services' titles may be purchased in
bulk quantities for educational, fund-raising,
business, or promotional use.
bulksales@TEACHServices.com

Finally, if you are interested in seeing
your own book in print, please contact us at:
publishing@TEACHServices.com
We are happy to review your manuscript at no charge.

www.ingramcontent.com/pod-product-compliance
Lightning Source LLC
Chambersburg PA
CBHW062012180426
43199CB00034B/2471